HOW TO
BE HAPPY

Finding a Future in Your Past

First published by O Books, 2008
O Books is an imprint of John Hunt Publishing Ltd., The Bothy, Deershot Lodge, Park Lane, Ropley,
Hants, SO24 0BE, UK
office1@o-books.net
www.o-books.net

Distribution in:	South Africa
	Alternative Books
UK and Europe	altbook@peterhyde.co.za
Orca Book Services	Tel: 021 555 4027 Fax: 021 447 1430
orders@orcabookservices.co.uk	
Tel: 01202 665432 Fax: 01202 666219	Text copyright Jenny Smedley 2008
Int. code (44)	
	Design: Stuart Davies
USA and Canada	
NBN	ISBN: 978 1 84694 150 4
custserv@nbnbooks.com	
Tel: 1 800 462 6420 Fax: 1 800 338 4550	All rights reserved. Except for brief quotations
	in critical articles or reviews, no part of this
Australia and New Zealand	book may be reproduced in any manner without
Brumby Books	prior written permission from the publishers.
sales@brumbybooks.com.au	
Tel: 61 3 9761 5535 Fax: 61 3 9761 7095	The rights of Jenny Smedley as author have
	been asserted in accordance with the
Far East (offices in Singapore, Thailand,	Copyright, Designs and Patents Act 1988.
Hong Kong, Taiwan)	
Pansing Distribution Pte Ltd	
kemal@pansing.com	A CIP catalogue record for this book is available
Tel: 65 6319 9939 Fax: 65 6462 5761	from the British Library.

Printed by Chris Fowler International
www.chrisfowler.com

HOW TO BE HAPPY

Finding a Future in Your Past

Jenny Smedley

BOOKS

Winchester, UK
Washington, USA

CONTENTS

ABOUT ME

In 1995 I had reached a crossroads in my life. As a recurrent depressive I had reached the point where I either gave up my life, which I felt was over, or found some way to energize myself. The depression was inexplicable because there was no apparent reason for it, and yet even my much loved husband had been unable to help me shake it off. I was overweight, and I felt, totally without any useful talents. I felt that at 45, my life was over, with nothing ahead but a downhill slide. I searched desperately, and sought for something to give my life meaning, but to no avail. I had read of people who had their lives 'changed in a second', and never really believed it was possible, and yet that was exactly what happened to me one afternoon.

An experience that happened in the space of a few seconds opened my eyes to one of my past lives, and in those seconds everything changed. (See Souls Don't Lie – O Books). My depression not only went for that moment, but was entirely banished. Over the next few months I rediscovered the whole of my being, by recognizing who I had been in another lifetime. This realization led me to understanding my purpose in this life, and once that happened and I accepted it, I was given the tools to succeed.

In the next few years I lost 45 lbs without starving myself, became an award-winning lyricist, achieved a job as a daily TV presenter on Taunton TV, overcame a phobia of flying, lost a debilitating abdominal pain, became an author, and finally achieved my lifetime goal of earning a living through writing. But more than any of those things, I became *happy*.

As long as you are not aware of the continual law of Die and Be Again, you are merely a vague guest on a dark Earth.

Johann Wolfgang von Goethe, (German poet, playwright and scientist)

I died as a mineral and became a plant, I died as a plant and rose to animal, I died as animal and I was man. Why should I fear? When was I less by dying?

Jalalu Rumi (Islamic Poet of the 13th century)

Coming and going, people wander through reincarnation; they act according to their past actions.

Sri Guru Granth Sahib

Just when the caterpillar thought the world was over, it turned into a butterfly.

Unknown

Happiness depends upon ourselves.

Aristotle (384 BC - 322 BC)

Dedications

This book is dedicated to every person who ever wrote to me for advice about their past lives.

It is a tribute to my husband, soul mate and best friend, Tony.

And it's a big thank you to all the past life therapists who have helped me with research.

*If I'd been asked some years ago if there was any one person
I really missed having in my life,
I would have said, yes, the person I thought I would be by now.*

*If you feel the same way, then this book could tell you how to release
that person.*

CHAPTER 1

What good does it do to look into your past?

"I've enough problems in this life, without adding to them with problems I had in past lives!" I've often had these words thrown at me by people who would very likely benefit by looking into their own distant history. If you're someone who might have protested like that, then you probably think that by finding out about your past problems, you'll only add to the ones you already know about from this lifetime. But in fact quite the reverse is true. Problems from today are invariably *caused* by those in our past, and therefore our current problems have the potential to be healed by understanding the past. It's an ongoing situation.

Understanding the progression of your soul, and 'observing the scenarios' that led you to where you are today, enables you to make sense of it all and move forward with confidence and direction. Rather than adding to your current problems, remembering the unfinished business and emotional battle scars from past life traumas and hang-ups, can resolve them. Understanding *why* your problems of today exist, gives you the means to re-write your current life to a different, more palatable, script.

The problems you bring through may encompass relationship issues, a run of 'bad luck', career problems, health issues, a feeling that something is missing, depression, weight problems, phobias, obsessions, family disputes, compulsions, nightmares, ghosts – the list is endless!

The reason that recalling past lives can resolve these problems is that remembering them helps you understand why you act and think the way you do, and why you're going through what you're going through today. Truly understanding yourself is paramount. Knowledge really is power. Past lives are often responsible for glitches in your psyche. Regression to past lives, and re-living key experiences, gives you an opportunity to heal traumas and open up your current life to different behaviour patterns, removing destructive, self-sabotaging habits.

Your Master Plan – that which you came into this life to accomplish, and so essential to create any feeling of fulfillment, can suddenly be revealed to an open mind that has knowledge. Only by fulfilling this master plan will you find true happiness (that which comes from *inside you*), and achieve your full potential.

Happiness that comes from inside, *cannot* be destroyed by outside events. Of course you'll still experience problems, because no one's life is 100% perfect 100% of the time, but the problems you encounter won't be able to destroy that inner core of deep happiness, the knowing that you're here for a purpose.

Making sense of life goes a very long way to enabling you to enjoy every moment of it. Once you take a step on your rightful path, with the right state of mind, other things will unblock and fall into place. Doors once closed will open, and difficulties that once seemed insurmountable will fade away.

The secret of happiness and curing 'bad luck' is inside each and every one of you. So-called 'bad luck' comes because you have some lessons to learn. Lessons, once understood, will be removed from your path, and guidance, once accepted, will put you on the road to a happy future. You must go back into your own history in order to understand your lessons. You must accept guidance so that you can walk forward with trust that you will be led to the right place. By seeking help to remember the lives that have shaped your current one, you can achieve both these things.

*

During my role as past life advisor in magazine columns, in books, and on television and radio, I've witnessed many hundreds of past life regressions. These have varied from those done under hypnosis, by myself or by other therapists, by self-hypnosis, and through the use of my Past Life Meditation CD.

I'm always swamped with requests for help, and can't possibly deal with every single one on a one-to-one basis, so I have to be selective. Out of the many hundreds of people who write to me, I choose which people to help personally, based on the particular and well-defined problems they're experiencing, selecting the most common-place past life 'carry-overs', so that their problems and the resolution of them will help as wide a field of readers as possible.

It has been fascinating to see how once people re-experience these logical scenarios that explain everything they feel is wrong with their current life, they are able to have secure relationships, where before there was only hurt, mistrust and confusion. They feel safer and more secure in their everyday lives and family situations, whereas before they felt only doubt and danger. They are able to understand their own personality, whereas before they were a complete mystery to themselves.

In the following chapters you'll see how people from all walks of life, suffering from all kinds of very common problems, were able to see themselves in a whole new light. Understanding and rationalizing previously inexplicable feelings of deep guilt and lack of self-worth have been replaced by feelings of contentment and a belief that each person deserves to be happy.

Removing unnecessary guilt from the person's mind is a truly miraculous way to release them from a life of torment. Even more amazing, once the soul is cleansed in this way, people are able to see clearly, often for the first time, how they have been creating their own punishment and apparent misfortune in a misguided attempt to atone for a crime they did not even remember committing.

Some people have asked me, "if these memories are so important to us, why don't we remember automatically and save ourselves from all this misery?"

That very conundrum *is* the challenge. You come here fragmented, mind and soul split apart, in mortal form, subject to all the trials, hurts and tribulations of being human. You come to experience all that you can *only* experience in physical bodies, and at the same time you accept the challenge of reuniting your mind and soul. If you can overcome all that life throws at you, all the ways that parents and peers, bosses and teachers, partners and offspring, misguidedly use to change you and shape you to fit into society, without losing your real 'shape', you have a chance of succeeding.

If you can endure all this and still find your way back to a spiritual unity, then you will have overcome the odds and beaten the challenge you set yourself.

Winning in this way leads you on to a greater spiritual plane. Failing in this task and continuing to make the same mistakes, without ever looking for, or finding the reasons, leads you back to the cycle, back onto the merry-go-round that you call life. Until you succeed in seeing your whole self for the first time, you will continue going round and round, repeating the same mistakes, often with the same group of people.

Somewhere in the following pages you'll recognize aspects of yourself, and the problems you're struggling with, which will lead you on a voyage of self-discovery. Welcome to the journey of your lives.

CHAPTER 2

Relationships: Soul Mates

You often meet someone and just 'know' that they're your soul mate, and yet shockingly, what sometimes happens is that a lot further down the road, you suddenly find that you're upset and disbelieving, because things have totally and inexplicably, fallen apart. Your 'soul mate' has suddenly turned away from you, sometimes after giving you a child, and seems to have changed beyond recognition.

There's often still love between you, which makes the situation even more hurtful. Both of you still love each other in your own way, and yet living together becomes impossible. You're lost, puzzled, bruised and simply don't know what's gone wrong. The estranged partner will classically, when asked why they've left you, have absolutely no answer to give you. This generates more hurt in you because you need some sort of explanation as to why this person has suddenly stopped being there for you. At this stage you may start blaming yourself, which leads to problems in any future relationships.

You and the person you thought was with you for life, may even sleep together again on occasion, which fosters hopes of reconciliation in you, but when asked the partner says no, things haven't changed and has only vague answers, nothing to ease the pain.

The reason this happens is that what the two of you felt on meeting, while real in its way, was not the everlasting commitment you thought it was. Rather, what you felt was familiarity, comfort, and a sense of 'rightness'. These three things added together are easily mistaken for that often misunderstood emotion, 'love'.

Real love *is* never-ending, and someone who loves another truly, will be incapable of inflicting hurt or unfaithfulness on the other, or of voluntarily leaving the one they love. This is true simply because two real 'lovers' are as one person, not soul mates, but twin souls, one a half of the other. To inflict hurt on or abandon this kind of partner is just like inflicting it on yourself, so if you hurt the 'one you love' or they hurt you in a way that was preventable, through disloyalty, then the two of you are not in love in this lifetime, no matter how much you may think it feels like it. And if either of you is willing to chance the other one's heart being broken, just for a ten minute thrill from sexual inter-action with another physical body, then you certainly don't love them in the true sense of the word.

What you two, who felt so right when you met, experienced in the beginning is not love but *recognition* that you already know the other person (from a past life). You felt comfort, especially if this person was for example, a reliable partner or parent in a previous incarnation. You felt a sense of rightness, and in some cases this may be because you made a contract to be with this person for a time. When this happens it's usually in order that you should create a certain child that needed both your genes. Once the child is born, or the joy of mere comfort becomes insufficient, one of the two of you will get strong signals to leave, from their higher self, but will often not know why they're getting this irresistible message. All the particular partner knows is that they must leave.

In that case, unless you research your relationship's distant past life history you won't know that you or they may be leaving to make way for the possibility of a twin soul to come into the other person's life.

Why did he do that to me?

Clare, who was 32, came to me with a problem like this. She was terribly fragile emotionally and couldn't see why her husband, Kevin, had left her and their three children, just after the youngest daughter was born. The worst thing was that Kevin couldn't give her any real reason for this sudden and devastating change of heart. He had remained loving in attitude but had simply repeated over and over that he just had to leave. He said he needed space, and yet continued to visit a lot. He still loved Clare and the children, but insisted he had to go. He was very willing to uphold his parental responsibilities, but could not live in the family home any longer. On more than one occasion Kevin stayed the night with Clare, only to leave, quite coldly, in the morning. This roller coaster left Clare shattered emotionally.

When questioned closely before regression, Clare admitted there had never been what she called physical 'fireworks' between her and Kevin, but she didn't think that really mattered very much. She had relied on him, had thought he loved her, and had felt betrayed, bereft and abandoned by his decision to end the relationship.

Clare's regression revealed the reasons for events in this life and her apparent abandonment. During this regression Clare spoke in an accent with a manner far removed from her normal East London brogue, a phenomenon that does happen quite often in regressions.

This account and those that follow have been related in the first person, just as it happened, and the therapists' questions to their clients have been removed to make it easier to read and understand. Incidentally, questions put forward by an experienced and skilled therapist should always be open, and not leading or prompting in any way. For instance, one should be asked, "Where are you?" rather than "Are you inside?"

Clare: *It's quite dark. The flickering light is only from candles and a log fire. Shadows edge the margins of the lofty-walled room. All is silent save the spitting of the fire and creaks and groans from the timbers above. The wind is getting up now though and its fingers quest through the draughty window frames, making a spooky, moaning noise. But my* husband, Gerald is here and so all is well. I am wearing a heavy velvet dressing gown over my nightclothes, a cap pulled down over my curls. Suddenly, our peace is broken by a loud hammering on the outer door. I am startled, but Gerald merely stretches lazily, like a cat, and he gets up to answer the summons. He never panics! He is my rock, my protector. When he comes back in, his brother, Simeon is with him.

Simeon is very different to Gerald. My husband is brawny, dark and tall. When we walk through the town together I feel safe from any attack, of which there is great danger. Only a fool would attack him or anyone under his protection. He provides for us and our children very well. He's a good man.

Simeon is dark and tall, but slight of build. When he walks into the room with Gerald, he looks like his brother's mere shadow, a wraith of the original. Simeon is a dreamer, unreliable. He drifts through his life relying on handouts from his older brother. And yet, he is attractive to me.

The very first time I met him, just before Gerald and I were wed, I was drawn to him. There was some kind of magnetic attraction between us. His body calls to mine in a way that Gerald's never has. My pulse quickens when Simeon accidentally brushes against me. It's a feeling I have to subdue for decency's sake.

I have never really regretted my choice in Gerald, although I will admit I feel a little wistful in Simeon's presence sometimes. There is something about him that makes me feel different to how I feel towards his so solid brother. Simeon is dangerous I think, but not in the muscular way that Gerald is.

Simeon has brought news of the war. It seems the Scots are winning battle after battle, while our men flee like children before them. I know what is coming. My husband will say, 'Enough! I am going to join the fight!' and Simeon will talk him out of it, making light of it, as always, thank God. I could not survive without the children's father. Simeon has a silver tongue and even Gerald can't resist it.

Perhaps even I could not resist it…but he has no thoughts of me. Simeon's lust lies in a direction I cannot compete with, even should I *want to. Gerald has told me in whispered tones that his brother loves another man and does not seek the company of women. It is never spoken of aloud, but it is always in my mind when I see him.*

Some Years Later

I am bloody, dying. A band of screaming, bloodstained men battered their way into the house hours ago. My rock, my husband, my defender, was not here. I have been assaulted, wounded, and my children have been taken. I can no longer hear their cries. My children! My poor children. I'll never see them again. I have been stabbed. There is little pain now, and I know my breaths will be few. My mind tries to take me on a fantasy of what might have been had I chosen differently, and yet all I can see is Simeon in the arms of another man. I choke.

The door opens and Simeon walks in. Seeing me lying there bloody, he rushes to my side and falls to his knees. He is crying, but my ears are buzzing and I cannot hear what he says. His lips seem to be mouthing the words, 'I wish...I wish'. I wish too and I try to say something. My voice a harsh croak, I finally manage to say, 'Gerald told me, you love only men...you could never have loved me.' As my eyes close in death, the last thing I see is Simeon's face twist in grief and horror, 'No! No!' are the last words I hear.

I am going into the light and at last I feel more peace than I have ever known in life.

*

This past life memory, of a lifetime which took place in the 1640s near Glamorgan, explained everything to Clare. She knew that Kevin had been Gerald, and that in the life they shared back then he had lied about his brother being a homosexual, because he could see that there was an undeniable attraction between Simeon and his wife. Simeon had loved 'Clare', but out of brotherly loyalty he'd never told her. She had loved him, but had thought there could never be a relationship between them because of the lie her husband told her. Gerald had been a great husband in all other respects, as has Kevin, and she had always felt safe and comforted by him, just as she did now.

Looking at it from a clairvoyant viewpoint I could see that 'Simeon' was soon to enter Clare's life in her current incarnation, and that subconsciously Kevin knew this.

In this life he was going to step aside, because otherwise 'Simeon' would again feel unable to make a play for Clare as a married woman, and the love Clare and he should have had would be stifled again. It was an act of love of a sort.

Clare and Kevin had also made a contract in between that life and this one, to recreate their children, so that Clare could be with them again. This applied especially to their youngest daughter, a crystal child, one of many who will change this world for the better. Now that she was born, Kevin was free from his obligations to stay with Clare, and ready to live up to the other part of the pact. This time he would not stand between the twin souls.

Kevin will always be part of Clare's soul clan – that group we return to and interact with time after time. Perhaps Gerald would have met a partner he loved more deeply, if not for clinging to 'Clare', so tightly. In this life Kevin would be able to shrug off the mantle of guilt he wears for the lies he told as Gerald, if he too had a regression session. In this lifetime Kevin and Clare were not meant to be together forever, and now they can both move forward with confidence.

Clare: The hurt I felt has gone at last, and I am able to let go of Kevin, with love. This will be so much better for our children's relationship with their dad. Having experienced the unrequited love I felt for Simeon in that past life, I can't wait now for him to arrive in this one. I'm busy healing and clearing myself, ready for him. Life has become exciting. I've no doubt he will come, because I know he's real. Anything less than reality couldn't have made such a change in me, or in my outlook on life.

*

The Other Side of the Coin
Then you get the other side of the coin. You and your partner might really love each other very much, but while both of you feel you are soul mates, one of you has doubts that the feeling will last forever. One of you is happy and contented and confidently determined to make the relationship work, while the other one constantly wonders how long it'll last and looks for signs that cracks are appearing. Your opposing feelings make both of you anxious and sometimes angry. The two of you really *are* soul mates, and meant to be together till death in this lifetime, but obstacles and subconscious memories from your past lives together are in danger of ripping your situation apart.

Manifesting abandonment
Paula doubted that she and her husband, Michael, would ever be really happy. She was certain that he should be her soul mate, and yet she worried all the time that he would leave her. 'How could that be, if we were really soul mates?' she asked. She felt terrible suspicion and her self-confidence was very low. Soul mate or not, she didn't understand how Michael could elicit such feelings of imminent abandonment in her if it wasn't a reality waiting to happen. Infidelity was written prominently in her subconscious. She felt it was bound to happen, whatever she did. This, and the fear that she couldn't conceive a child, made her inescapably certain that the marriage was doomed to failure in the end. Michael could never be seen talking to another woman without Paula over-reacting, any mention of female work colleagues would send her into a jealous spiral of anger and hopelessness. This is what her regression revealed:

Paula: *I'm pretty, very pretty, and I know it. I use it. I'm smug inside. I've had many lovers. No boy has ever turned me down. I play with their*

*hearts, I torment them, and I enjoy the game. My name is Gertrude –
Gertie, as they all call me, and I work at the big house in
Wolverhampton. The Master, John Gifford, has his eye on me, and his
hands if he has the chance! Micky, the stable-lad loves me – really loves
me I think. At least that's the way it seems when he rolls with me in the
hay. Sometimes I think Micky and I could have something different,
some kind of love that is pure and untouchable, but the Master has what
Micky does not – money, and a way to give me a wonderful life. With
Micky, life would be too tough.*

Later

*I'm so scared. Oh God, I'm pregnant. I don't know what to do! I never
thought this would happen to me. Countless men have bedded me but I
never got pregnant. I thought I couldn't get pregnant. The baby is
Micky's. It has to be, because the Master, though he thinks he has lain
with me, was really always too drunk, and never stayed awake past a bit
of fumbling. He woke naked in my arms and I always led him to believe
he had been a great man. I never told him that he didn't succeed in
bedding me, and he's too vain to suspect that he didn't manage it.*

*Micky wants to marry me, God bless him. I do love him, at least I
think I love him, but what kind of life would it be for us and for the child
on a stable-lad's pay? I'd be dismissed from service too, no doubt once
the Master found out he'd been cuckolded. Micky says money doesn't
matter, that love will find a way, and he'll protect us and care for us
somehow. Silly boy!*

Later

*I went to the Master and told him I was with child, by him. He believed
me – stupid old man! Today we're to be married. Folk tell me I'm lucky
– that most gentry would have disowned me, but like I said, I'm very
pretty, and I know how to use it.*

*Micky was heartbroken, and I feel bad. He disappeared the day I told
him of my betrothal, and folk say he's done himself in. I miss him…but,
well, if he has, more fool him. My life is going to be good. If he chose to*

throw his away, then maybe he was right.

Later

I'm getting old. I only ever had the one child and it was stillborn. My life hasn't been so wonderful after all. I've been so lonely with only an old man for company. In any case, John's been dead many years now, and it's been very strange being the mistress, where once I was servant. None of the servants like me, and they blame me for Micky's disappearance.

I sometimes wish I could turn back the clock. I wonder if the baby would have lived, if I'd done the right thing. But I thought I was doing that. The right thing for me and for the baby. Not for Micky though. Maybe I would have been happier with him and not the money.

Paula: (Oh, I realized. Michael was Micky!)

*

It was a simple tale, but it changed Paula's life. She could see why infidelity was in her subconscious. It was because *she* had been unfaithful, in the past. Maybe she thought this time round it would be Michael's (Micky's) turn. Revenge served cold, years and years later, in another lifetime. But as I explained to her, that wasn't the case at all. She had come here to make amends, both to Micky, and to her then unborn child. I told her than what she actually had in this life was a second chance. She could make it up to Micky and get it right for herself this time. She could relax. Michael wasn't about to make the same mistake that Gertie had.

So in this case the two of them *were* meant to be together, and could be, happily so, once their past was revealed. The lesson of trust is a hard one to learn, but once she had succeeded, Paula would unblock many aspects of her life. She had Michael to teach her forgiveness too. Paula and Michael are still married. They're happy, and three months after the regression Paula fell pregnant with the first of two children.

*

Paula: The feelings I had were obviously guilt at what *I'd* done in a past life, and I'd transferred them to poor Michael. Thank goodness I was regressed because otherwise I was about to do him a great injustice – again. I feel calm and relaxed now, and safe in his love. All during our relationship I'd been certain that one day he'd do the dirty on me, I'd almost pushed him into it. But in fact, I was the unfaithful type, not him.

CHAPTER 3

Destructive Relationships

In this situation you and your partner seem determined to destroy each other, it's as if your relationship is some sort of competition. You're constantly reeling from being hurt, or gloating over scoring a hit on the other person, yet you never consider parting. You feel as if you have to be on top all the time, and the only way to guarantee that is to put your partner down. You seem tied together.

Friends advise you to split up and find someone better for yourself, but both of you insist you love each other. Yet you criticize each other in front of people, and embarrass all your friends with your public bickering. You argue over the smallest triviality, and there's no support for either of you, from the other. To outsiders you seem to disagree all the time.

Why do you stay together? Is this love? Is there any hope for you? Should you stay together? The answers very often, are surprisingly, yes it is, yes there is, and yes you should.

Master and Mistress

Josie and Jack came to me with just such a problem. Josie loved her partner Jack, very much, she said, but wanted him to be more supportive. She said he was dismissive of her emotions and made her feel inadequate. Yet she loved him. Sex between them was explosive, even after five years of marriage, and although she admitted that their arguments, or rather the 'making up' fuelled this part of the relationship, she did long for him to be more tender sometimes.

Jack, for his part, said that he felt Josie should show more of her feminine side, and should be more supportive of him in his career. She should be more compliant and surrender to his masculinity sometimes. Neither one was interested in leaving or finding a new partner, but they knew they couldn't go on indefinitely as they were.

The answers, when they were both regressed and exchanged notes afterwards, amazed them. Both of their multiple stories have been merged here, but most points made by one were corroborated by the other.

Josie: *I'm a servant, a 'nobody', little more than a slave, on a plantation, in Green County, Georgia [America]. My name is Sara – that's not my born name, I barely remember that.*

My black skin is a license for people to treat me like an animal. I don't know what it's like to rest. Dawn till dark I have to do everything I'm asked. It doesn't end there. My Master treats me like his property in every possible way. I have to accept whatever he wants. I'm helpless.

Jack: *I'm called Stephen Channing. I care about my slaves, unlike some. I clothe them and stop them congregating at night because they catch diseases too often that way. They're little more than beasts, but I treat them better than most. Especially Sara.*

I have a soft spot for Sara. Her black skin is like satin and her eyes gleam in the dark. I think she likes me, as much as an animal can like a human being. She enjoys my attention.

Next life

Josie: *I've taken a dislike to George. It's not that he's not a hard worker, but something about him, the way he looks at me. He's insolent. I give him the dirtiest jobs, the hardest work. I feel a need to make him weary, so that his mind stays pure. He's German, and George isn't his real name, but I refuse to pronounce that guttural German-speak, so George he'll be till he dies. The colonies need indentured servants. We couldn't run the houses without them and that's the only reason I tolerate his presence. He has his uses.*

Jack: *I hate my mistress, a harridan and despot! She looks at me with daggers in her eyes, as if I lusted after her. She might be a beautiful woman but she has a mean and vicious heart. Nothing's ever good enough for her. She enjoys hurting people. There is no love in her. When she called me to her boudoir this night I was shocked and afraid. But I can deny her nothing if I want to stay alive.*

Next Life

Josie: *I'm only 14 years old and an under stairs maid to a Thai family. I can't stand this place. It's so hot and humid. I long for an English winter. Season changes. Here it's always the same, wet and hot and sweaty. The mistress isn't too bad, but the Master likes to have his way with me when she's out. I won't live long here. The work is so hard and the sweat pours off me all day and all night. I'm skin and bone. I get beaten daily.*

Now I'm pregnant and I'm terrified. It will be the end of me. Some part of me is glad. Soon it will all be over. Death is the only way out of this sorry life.

Jack: *My name is Kasam and I am master of my own home and all who live in it. The little white-skinned maid, Lily, is mine to use as I see fit, despite what my wife might think. Lily's parents put her into my service and I'm hopeful she will give me many children to carry on the family name. My wife is incapable of bearing a son. Lily's son will be brought up as ours.*

*

The regressions didn't need to go any further as the problem was obvious. It was a vicious cycle. People get trapped on these all the time. Each life they come in, determined to put everything right this time and finally move on, but the grudges from their pasts are so deeply embedded in their psyche that once here in human form, they can't see any other way than to continue tit-for-tat, life after life. Vengeance takes over from common sense, and their life once more becomes a battlefield of words, from which neither will ultimately emerge a winner.

Life after life, Jack and Josie had been playing out the master/mistress/slave/servant scenarios. It may have started with Sara's miserable life, so it would be easy to blame Jack for the competition that had been going on ever since. However, he was just a victim of his own upbringing, as we mostly are. He was taught to believe that slaves were just animals to be used, and he did believe it. He did take some steps to take care of them, and was kindly in his own way, for that time in history. It was time for Josie to forgive him for that first lifetime, and realize that ever since then they had been coming back together to put things right. But instead, they had continued the fight, each one trying to dominate the other. In this lifetime, they were equal, as men and women should be today, as all races and all classes should be today, so they had turned to emotional put downs instead of physical. Their sex-life was so fiery because subconsciously they were playing out their master/slave fantasies. The only thing is, for them they weren't fantasies but memories.

*

Josie: Oh, this explained everything to me. It's made us stronger because we now see how we've been stuck going round and round, when we are actually a partnership, trying to right a wrong, and failing spectacularly. No more though, now we understand what we're here for, and we're going to work together to achieve it. We're both very strong individuals, so once we start playing as a team we'll be unbeatable.

Jack: I feel very guilty about the past. But I have to get through that. Those acts weren't committed by me, or by Josie, but in this lifetime I have to take responsibility for my actions. I really love her and from now on I'm going to act that way. I think we'll even role play some of our previous lives in the bedroom. If we do that but turn the tables on each other at the same time, I think we'll heal and have a great time to boot!

*

Why doesn't he see me as a lover?
Sue and Greg had a different problem. They felt tied together, definitely meant to be together forever, but Sue said that no matter how she tried, she felt there was a block between them, a wall. Greg said that despite having children, he always felt Sue was withholding in their lovemaking, as if she felt it was dirty somehow. In his turn he had trouble seeing her as a sexual partner, and Sue complained that he treated her more like the mother of his children and not like a lover. Intimacy was difficult between them. Sex was always a tense selfish affair, neither one of them fully giving to the other and it would surely not be long before one of them looked elsewhere for what they felt was lacking.

Their regressions gave all the answers they were looking for, and in a way they could never have dreamed.

Sue: *I'm wearing a crinoline dress all puffed up with petticoats and pretty sparkly slippers. I feel wonderful, and yet there is sadness around me. I'm all alone in the world. I never knew my family as I was sent away when I was very small. I can vaguely remember a farm and some older boys that I was very fond of. People tell me that the whole village was dying of a plague and I was sent away to save me. My brothers, Francis and Joseph stayed behind to help farm the land.*

Later
I never heard from my brothers again, until today that is. Suddenly I've discovered that I still have some family living. They've been in the

village all this time, while I thought everyone there was dead. I'm in a coach, going back to the old village to meet them. The trip will take just three days and I'm both scared and excited at the same time, and I'm 18 years old today.

Greg: *We haven't seen our little sister, Maria, since she was five. Plague came to our village and our parents decided to send her to distant relatives for her own sake. The relatives were wealthy and they took her in as their own. We were never allowed to make contact, because we weren't thought good enough to mix with that branch of the family. Our sister might as well have been dead to us. But now, we are waiting for her to arrive back in the village. It was thirteen years ago that she left. She'll be a fine lady, too high and mighty to talk to us much, I expect. She has been far removed from our humble birth. It wasn't until her adoptive parents died that we heard from her at all. I hope she's not going to offer us charity. I doubt she'll even know us, or us her.*

Sue: *The coach pulls up. My heart is pounding. I see two young men waiting for me. Big, strong and handsome they are. Can this be Francis and Joseph? I recognize the village and the small stone houses. I feel over-dressed in my finery. I hope they can see that I'm still me under all this.*

Greg: *Oh my, she's very beautiful. I never expected that. Dark curled hair, sparkling green eyes, and her clothes. I can't move. I can't get any closer. How can I touch this lady with my rough and dirty hands? I scrubbed and scrubbed them but the soil is ingrained into my skin. I stop and wait to see if she will acknowledge us.*

To my amazement, she's crying, she calls out, "Francis! Oh Francis! Joseph! My brothers!" She's running towards us, arms out-stretched. Her hair and dress are flying in the wind and her little ankles are flashing as her skirt lifts. I'm so happy. She does know us. She does want to be our sister again. I open my arms to catch her, then suddenly there's a bang, an explosion of sound, and I'm on the ground on my face. There's mud in my mouth and I can't breathe. Maria drops to her knees beside me. I've been shot. I can feel cold pain and the hot flow of blood. That madman, Lucas, our crazy neighbor, he said he'd kill me but I didn't believe him...It's going black. I can't see.

Sue: *Oh no, I can't believe it. My older brother, my hero, restored to me after all this time, to be snatched away so cruelly. He lies dead on the ground at my feet. I wanted time to know him again, and now I have lost him forever.*

*

Francis and Maria had been brother and sister; the brother hero-worshipped for years from afar by Maria, while all the while Francis thought Maria, his sister, was changed and would be too good for the likes of him. Add to that the sudden, violent death that tore them apart before they could reconcile and understand that each of them loved the other, and it's no wonder they had very confused feelings for each other in this lifetime when they became partners.

Sue: No wonder I felt like I did, no wonder I felt a wall between us. Maria had loved her brother from afar for so long. She didn't really know him, and just as she was about to, he was snatched from her. I think maybe I'm afraid subconsciously that if I give myself to Greg too completely, he might be taken away again. That it's better to keep him at arm's length, as Francis was kept from me, because as soon as I was near to him, he died. Also, yes, that feeling of sister and brother has come through to a certain extent. I have to change my love to that of loved and lover instead. Maybe if Francis and Maria had been given time together, to get to know each other as brother and sister, we wouldn't have felt such constriction between us in this life. Bodies are, after all, just envelopes, so I needn't feel that sex with

Greg is wrong in any way.

Greg: I can see now why I always felt Sue was too ladylike to be my lover, and also that I had to be on my best and gentlest behaviour with her. It also explains why she might have felt lovemaking between us wasn't right, her having been my sister before. I held back from showing my passion, so she thought I didn't really love her, while all the time I actually worshipped her, too much. She doesn't want worshipping, she wants loving, plain and simple. I think we can get past this problem now, because now I'm able to see her as a woman first, above everything else. Maria didn't think she was above me despite my fears as Francis, so there's no reason I should have felt that Sue was above me either. She doesn't need reverence; she needs real and physical affection.

CHAPTER 4

Relationship Problems: Abusive and Unsupportive Partners

How wonderful you feel. You found Mr Right (OR Miss Right). He's strong, manly, passionate, and he can't get enough of you, and he seems perfect. Or she's sweet, pretty, loving and supportive, everything you ever dreamed of in a woman. But a few months into the relationship you find out that he or she is actually Mr (or Mrs) Hyde. It wouldn't be so bad, but this is the third time you've done this. You just keep making the wrong choices. Why is it that everyone else seems to end up with a Prince or Princess Charming, and all you get is a frog? No amount of kissing will change things either. You've tried that. He/she has become disrespectful, abusive, critical, maybe even violent, and you think – *maybe it's me.* You think *it's always the same. Maybe I don't know how to be good for anyone, and they'll all turn out this way. I'm going to end up alone.*

You're right in that this is actually a repeating cycle, but it goes back much further than you think. It goes right back into your distant history. There are usually two reasons for this to keep happening in this life and in life after life. Either you're carrying guilt from past lives, which makes you feel you don't deserve gentleness and consideration, and so you choose men or women who you know (subconsciously) won't give it to you. This is self-punishment.

The other cause can be that there is unfinished business from past lives, involving all these same people, and until you find out all the facts that created them, the sorry parade of unfulfilling scenarios are going to continue. But, there is hope. Once you under-stand why you're stuck creating this over and over, you can stop it.

Punishing herself

Sarah had been through this scenario at least five times and every time had turned out the same – badly. No wonder she was starting to give up on ever finding her soul mate. Her latest flame, and the one that had really burnt her badly, was Jason. He was definitely her type, tall, blond, good-looking, a cleft chin (they just *had* to have a cleft chin) rugged, and powerful looking. Physique meant an awful lot to her. Her friends had given up trying to help her find her perfect mate, because not one of the sweet and kind men they lined up ever matched her exacting criteria. She would totally ignore any dark-haired men, no matter how nice they were. And if they weren't muscle-bound, they didn't appeal to her. No, she went for that same look every time, over and above anything else, and every time it ended in disaster. Jason had turned out to be the same old cheating bully as the others, once he had snared her.

Her regression revealed some very interesting scenarios.

Sarah: *I'm wearing black, laced-up boots, a pair of tight breeches and a black, fitted jacket. I'm a man. I'm swaggering down a cobbled lane, and I feel very weird. So, this is how it feels to be a man. I'm walking differently, no hip sway, and there's that strange weight between my legs. I quite like the sensations though, I feel strong, and people are glancing at me with respect as I pass them by.*

My name is Conrad, and it's 1786. I'm on my way to the Black Bull on Romney Marshes. The village folk make way for me with deference, as well they might.

I'm hoping to meet little Rosie at the inn. She said she'd come. She'd better if she knows what's good for her. I'm at the inn. Ah, there she is, crouched by the fireside like a little mouse. She hates to come to the inn alone, it's 'not seemly' she says.

I insist. Haha! It amuses me to make her come here. Making her obey my wishes and not her own, puts her in the right frame of mind, makes her compliant and obedient, if you know what I mean. Makes her ready

to obey me in ways she might otherwise have resisted. Female humili-
ation turns me on.

Later

I've finished with Rosie, done for the night. She can get lost now. "Oh,
*don't you love me?" she simpers. Ha! I don't love anyone but **me**, and*
that's the way it will always be. She's annoying me now with her
sniveling and whining, and so I push her bodily from the bed, across the
room and out the door. She cries and sobs for me to let her get dressed
first. I can imagine how the 'mouse' would feel should she end up naked
on the streets, with all and sundry leering at her. That idea amuses me
so much that I almost make her do it. But it's arousing me, the thought
of men's eyes poring over her bare skin, with her frantically trying to
cover herself, so much so that I decide to let her back in to service me
again.

Later

I'm calling on Maggie now, the local whore. She's my kind of woman
sometimes, no questions, and no arguments. Just whatever I want her to
do, she does. It amuses me to play with the likes of Rosie now and again,
and make her squirm, but Maggie's safer. If my seed infects her, she
knows what to do, and there's no danger of her coming crying to me.
Every time with Rosie is a risk. Her father might be quite handy with a
shotgun. I'd have to leave the town, and I'm set up here real nice, so I
have to be careful.

Later

I'm furious! Some sniveling little man jumped on me as I came out of
Maggie's house. He was shouting and yelling at me about how I'd hurt
Rosie. How I was humiliating her by going with Maggie. He punched
me, but he was such a lightweight it made me laugh. I tormented him,
saying Maggie wasn't the only one. I told him that a real man would
never be satisfied with a little mouse like Rosie. Finally, I floored him,
kicked him and left him bleeding in the dust of the lane. Now I'm going

back to see to Rosie. She is going to be so sorry that she dared complain about me. By the time I've finished with her no man will ever look at her again.

*

It was pretty obvious that in her past life as Conrad, Sarah had been the very sort of bullying womanizer she kept saddling herself with in this lifetime. It was self-punishment. This was a mistake. The reason we come back here is *not* for punishment. That wouldn't be in any way productive. No matter what we did in the past, we come back again to learn, to experience *different* things, and Sarah hadn't learned anything. She'd got hung up on a cycle of 'making up' for what Conrad had done, by becoming 'Rosie' time after time after time. Conrad had been very fond of his own reflection in the mirror, which was tall, blond, good-looking, and yes, he had a cleft chin. Sarah needed to get over how Conrad had treated the women in his life, and start living the life she came here to live.

*

Sarah: So, all my life I've been punishing myself for the way I'd treated women, by hooking up with 'Conrads', and then letting them abuse me. Even if I'd still felt guilty for what Conrad did, which I accepted was unnecessary, I could have seen now that I'd been punished quite enough. I'd been turning down really nice blokes, vetted for temperament by my mates, just because they didn't look like Conrad, and were nice to me. It's going to stop right now. From now on I'll be looking at the men's hearts, not their hair or facial features. I can't believe how silly I've been.

*

Just cause?

Sam was the other extreme. He was a nice-looking guy, seemingly kind and apparently devoted to Tricia, his wife, but he had another, darker side that only Tricia ever saw, and this was what he wanted help with. He and Tricia had met, fallen in love and married, all within the space of six months. It had felt so right, he said. But a year down the line, things were getting rocky. He said there were times when Tricia would say the wrong thing, and a sudden and uncontrollable, red mist would descend. He was terrified that he would actually attack Tricia one day, and if that happened, he said, he wouldn't be able to live with himself. He was sure he loved her, but at those times of loss of control, the slightest thing would drive him into a blind, jealous rage.

Even more worryingly, this wasn't the first time he'd had this sort of trouble. He had once hit a girl just because she had danced with another guy, even though he hadn't been that keen on her. He said he'd had a terrible feeling of "Oh no, not again!" come over him, and that was what he'd reacted to, rather than a feeling of jealousy or possessiveness. Of course she had run a mile immediately, and Sam had managed to convince himself that it had been a one-off.

He hadn't hit his wife Tricia yet – but the mental abuse was well under way. He couldn't seem to help himself from putting Tricia down, especially in public, and afterwards he didn't have any answers as to why. It was as if he needed her to be nervous and lacking in confidence and self-esteem for some reason. When he made Tricia feel that way, it made him feel more confident and more in control of her.

Tricia had also had this happen before. She even felt there was something in her that liked her men to be tetchy and easily ruffled, as if she deserved it somehow, and yet it terrified her at the same time. She said she loved Sam more than life though, and really wanted to make it work, "whatever she had to put up with."

I already had an idea of what was going on here, but their past life confirmed it. They both used my past life CD independently in different rooms, and we compared notes afterwards. When it's done this way it gives remarkable confirmation that what both saw was factual.

Sam: *She's right in front of me, the most gorgeous thing I've ever seen. She's petite with an hour-glass figure, like a perfect doll. She has shoulder-length red curls that are usually bound up, but lie free on her skin right now. She's got the creamiest of skin and the bluest of eyes. I'd die for her. She's my wife, and I'm so lucky. We live in Sidmouth, and the year is 1899. We have a cottage and a small garden, and life is wonderful. I'll never want for anything.*

Tricia: *I'm bored, bored, bored! I'm tired of being adored. I want some excitement, but there never is any. The cottage is pokey and damp, and while my husband is out at work, I'm expected to just sit and sew and wait. Once a week I get to go to the butcher's shop to choose the week's meat, and joy, if I'm lucky, I get to flirt with Jimmy, the butcher's boy. He doesn't treat me like I'm made of glass. His hand on my back is firm and exciting. He's cheeky, and he makes me feel naughty. My husband makes me feel like a dull, old woman, to be revered and treated like I'll break if he squeezes me too hard.*

Later

Sam: *I can't believe it. I can't believe she did that to me, with a shop-keeper of all people! I came home early today and she was in our bed...our bed...with him. I'm disgusted, and I'm heart broken. I grab my pistol and run from the house. I could kill her, but what good would that do? I'd still feel as bad. I'm betrayed, a laughing stock and I can't go on with it. I'm out of breath, down by the railway line. I slump to the cold ground and cock the pistol. The noise of the steam train will drown out the sound of the gun. I like the idea of my body lying here, undiscovered, alone, abandoned…*

Tricia was totally horrified when she came out of the session. She couldn't believe she'd hurt Sam so badly in their past life, but she calmed down as I explained that this revelation should hold no guilt. The whole purpose of waking up to your past is to resolve it, not generate guilt. She had evolved upwards from that soul and she was no longer that person. What both she and Sam needed to do was sever themselves from that past and start again. Now that Sam knew why he got so angry and jealous, and now that Tricia knew what had happened to them both, healing could start to take place. However, Sam was still going to need to work on his anger, as his emotional receptors had become used to settling his issues with violence. He would need some help to wean them away from that automatic response – a bit like someone trying to give up smoking has to work to remove nicotine receptors from their brain cells.

Sam: I felt less guilty than I did for my temper, but I never wanted to feel that way again, and I certainly didn't want it to ever escalate, so I was advised by Jenny that I should attend anger management classes until we were all sure that the past had been healed. If not, the slightest setback could cause an irreversible rift between me and Tricia. I know now that she wouldn't do what she did back then as my wife. She's not going to cheat on me. That person was not Tricia, who I know now, and I really feel that I won't have any more trouble. Now that I know where my anger came from, and what caused it, I can understand that it isn't necessary in this lifetime.

Tricia: It was explained that I shouldn't take on any guilt burdens for that life, because it would be counter-productive, and not help matters at all. In fact it would generate a whole new setup of problems. Of course I certainly shouldn't accept Sam being aggressive to me either. I, Tricia, haven't cheated on anyone, so there was no need for me to accept punishment for it. But what it meant was that I could fully forgive Sam for his past outbursts, because I understood why they had happened. I needed to help him by making sure he knew that in this life I would never cheat on him, and wanted to make up for what had gone on in the past. I'm very happy because I always knew that Sam was my soul mate, and I'd have hated for this to have spilt us up. I feel more than ever now that we will be together, and happy, for the rest of our lives.

CHAPTER 5

Relationship Problems: Difficult Preferences

Some of you may think that all homosexuals are born that way, that it's natural to some people, and often that is the case. But what if you've always been a heterosexual, having had several partners of the opposite sex, and then suddenly you find yourself hopelessly and inexplicably falling in love with someone of the *same* sex? No other person of the same sex makes you feel the way this one does, and you can't believe you've suddenly become a homosexual, but what else can it mean?

Your parents and family and friends are mystified and quite possibly horrified by this turn of events, and look to you for answers, but you don't have any.

Soul connections and soul love can transcend time, gender, age, kinship, and any other hurdles put in its way. When a true soul connection is made, it's totally irresistible, and so, despite protests from friends and family, and even self-denial, you won't be able to break this bond that has flipped your entire life and belief system around. You'll feel like you just don't know yourself anymore and answers will be top of your list of priorities.

No Matter What

Rebecca and Chrissy had this problem. That they loved each other they had no doubt. Chrissy had always been an open lesbian and proud of who she was, but Rebecca couldn't understand why she was suddenly in love with another woman. Up until that point she'd always considered herself straight, and had looked forward to finding a husband and having a family. Now all that was changed and she was very confused. The relationship was faltering, despite their genuine love, because both were afraid that it wouldn't last, and Chrissy worried that Rebecca might suddenly become revolted by it. Chrissy was afraid it was a novelty for Rebecca that might fade with time, leaving her hurt and disillusioned. Rebecca was afraid that she could be turning her whole life and her perception of herself upside down for something that was a fluke, and bound not to last. But neither of them could contemplate life without the other one, so something had to be done. Unfortunately, Rebecca's family couldn't accept what had happened either. They were prejudiced against love between people of the same sex, and were horrified at this relationship, so they told Rebecca she had to choose between them or Chrissy. If she chose Chrissy Rebecca would lose her family and she'd possibly be giving up on having a family of her own. Yet they both truly loved one another, despite all the difficulties. But they wanted to know why.

The answers to everything came quite easily in the end. Rebecca and Chrissy were regressed separately, but the story revealed was the same.

Rebecca: *I'm a woman aged about 22 years. It's 1844, and a hot day. I'm hotter yet because I have a fever. I'm passing in and out of consciousness. Too weak to move much. Jack is with me, as always. He's sponging my burning skin with a wet towel. He's carried me out to the garden, where I love to be. I'm on a blanket in the shade of the oak tree. I can't feel any pain now, just the shuddering of the fever. Things are fading quite quickly and my vision is shrinking to a tunnel.*

Chrissy: *I'm Jack, Jack Hobbs. I'm so scared. I don't want to be alone, but there's no hope with this damn fever. Mary, my beautiful Mary, my wife, is lying on the blanket, sweating her life away, the tremors of the fever shaking her. I've never felt so helpless in my life. What will I ever do without her?*

Rebecca: *The fever is kind to me in a way. While Jack feels only fear, I am taken back in my mind to pleasant times, back through the years to our childhood. It was always Mary and Jack, since we were tots. We were always going to be married and live together forever. Forever seems to have ended too soon. I'm not long for this world. Jack is crying. I feel so helpless. I promised I'd never leave him. How will he cope alone?*

Chrissy: *I can't bear it. I promised I would love her forever, and take care of her. Love her forever I will, for sure, but take care of her? That's different. I can bathe her. I can keep the flies from her face. I can hold her in my arms, but I can't keep her safe. I can't hold her here, where I need her to be. I wish I could tell her how much she means. I don't think I ever did.*

Rebecca: *In my mind I'm in the past. I'm seeing our years together. We played together. We grew up together and our love grew into the adult kind. I'm wishing I could find words to tell Jack that I'll never leave him – how much I love him – how we'll be together again some day. But here in the present, where my body is, I haven't the strength to speak. The past unrolls before me and I so wish I'd put into words how I feel. I wish I hadn't left it too late.*

Chrissy: *The light is fading in her eyes. She's slipping away. I lean forwards, close to her ear and tell her. I tell her I'll always love her. I tell her I don't want to live without her. But I don't think she can hear me. I've left it too late. Her breathing slows, becomes shallow. Her breath on my cheek smells sweet still. Then that gentle breeze stops. There are no breaths. My love, my Mary, has left me.*

*

This was the unfinished business. Jack and Mary were both left feeling they hadn't declared their love in that lifetime. It was obvious that in spirit they had vowed to be together in this lifetime and not only that, but had made a contract that they would declare their love under the most difficult circumstances this time, no matter what, just to prove to each other how strong it was and had always been. Because Rebecca knew before she came to this life, that her family wouldn't accept her love for Chrissy (Jack), she knew she would need to show her love in a very strong way, against all odds, and this was what she wanted for Mary. She knew before she came here that she would face very strong opposition against her love for Jack (as Chrissy), and that the love would be tested to the limit for both of them. She knew that they would have to show the world that they did love each other with no doubts. This was what she wanted for Jack.

After the regressions, Rebecca and Chrissy declared their love for each other in the most public way, by getting married. Rebecca told her family that *they* were the ones that had to choose – that *she* had already chosen, centuries ago. She understood that love has no boundaries, not age, nor sex, nor race, and that it endured century after century. She told her family that she would have inevitably loved Chrissy, whether she had been man, boy, woman or girl; black, white or of any race or religion. That it would be impossible not to love her energy and spirit, whoever she had been and no matter what body her soul resided in. The family listened to the regression tapes with growing understanding, and they gradually came round to accepting the situation.

So Chrissy and Rebecca had yet another reason to bring their love through under those difficult circumstances. They taught their family members a little about love and respect. The family learned that real love can never be wrong, that everyone deserves to be loved and to be happy. Sometimes we come through with an apparently 'difficult' family for that very reason, because together we can learn something and teach each other something vital.

*

Forbidden Love

Sally and Christopher shared forbidden love of another sort. They were brother and sister. They'd been disowned by their families and left the place where they'd always lived. They had to do that because they believed they'd fallen in love with each other. There was chemistry between them that couldn't be denied, even though it was against the law for them to be together, and they'd never dare risk having any children together. It seemed they had little future together, but they didn't feel they could survive apart either.

Despite loving and feeling loved, and having moved to a community that didn't know they were incestuous, they still weren't happy. They didn't want to carry on the way they were, always being afraid of being discovered and feeling shame, even if only secretly and yet they were addicted to their love. They came to be regressed to see if they could find reasons for the way they felt, and a way to fight it.

Unusually, they insisted on being regressed together, apparently in case one found out something they felt a need to protect the other from, because they both wanted to know the whole story, warts and all. They wanted there to be no secrets. The regression was almost like a conversation – like I was watching a play unfold. Even in a trance they were still able to connect with each other.

Sally: *My name is Miriam. I'm very excited. John's been up in Scotland on business, and today his plane lands back here, at Newquay Airport. I've missed him so much. I hate to be parted from him. He gave up everything to be with me, and he took such risks. I'm so glad I found him.*

Christopher: *No, I didn't give up everything. Not my happiness. Anyway I gained so much. Miriam is my whole life now.*

Sally: *I'm so glad you're home. I've been so worried that my George (her* husband) *would come and take me away. I don't ever want to go back there. Back to him.*

Christopher: *I'd never let him take you. I'd die first. Our love is pure, of the purest kind, and nothing, not even his worst words can sully it.*

Later
By now Christopher was silent.

Sally: *Oh no, oh no, this can't be happening. My love, my one love, lies dead at my feet. George said he'd kill John if he ever found us. Now he's stabbed him. I don't want to live alone. I can't live with George. I'm sobbing as George grabs me and drags me away. No! Wait! John's not dead. He's moving. He's reaching out to me. I want to go to him, to hold him, but George drags me away. We live miles from anywhere. We don't have any visitors so no one will come to help him. This can't be. It can't be! I scream out to John! "I'll come back to you! I'll come back for you! I'll never leave you!"*

Later
Sally: *For the rest of my life, my whole life, I was George's prisoner. After trying desperately to escape for at least a month, and being caught and savagely beaten for every attempt, I finally gave up all hope of John still being alive. I knew then that no one had come and found him, because he never came for me. If he had lived nothing would have kept him from me. The rest of my life was endless misery without him.*

It seemed that Sally's last words to John in that life, and his to her, had lasting meaning to both of them. Sally's soul was devastated at being forced to leave John alone and dying. She promised to come back for him, but wasn't able to do so in that lifetime. She did it in this lifetime, but in a different way. Sally and John had pledged undying love for each other, and had contracted to be together in this life in some way that meant no one could steal the other away. As brother and sister they were certainly joined in a way that no one could sever, but it created difficulties they hadn't really anticipated. They had also sworn that their love was pure, above the physical, and had agreed that being brother and sister in this life would be the way to test and prove that to the world, and they felt they would be able to cope with the new relationship. While in spirit, it would have seemed a lot easier a proposition than it did once they were reincarnated in mortal form. Then it wasn't quite as easy as they'd imagined. They'd thought they could easily cope with a spiritual, soul level love only, one that didn't require a physical bond, but when it came to it, they wanted that too. Being brother and sister, and being told by their friends and family that it was wrong and unacceptable to intimately touch each other, couldn't prevent that need. It's still going to be a hard road for them, as it is for anyone who has taken a wrong turning, but knowing why they feel the way they do will, in time, help them gain control over it.

Sally: I can see now why we wanted to be partners, and why we maybe got confused. It still hurts, and I'm not going to be totally happy for some time yet, but at least I can see a way forward. At least I don't feel so guilty, now that I know we were once lovers, it stops me feeling that what we're doing and feeling is quite so unnatural. Because I understand why we have that feeling for each other, I can see where it's coming from, and that place isn't dirty.

Christopher: I don't really know what the future holds. I love Sally so much, but now I do feel the faintest start of a gentle separation, as if maybe I could settle for the fact that we did at least have that love once, and that at least in this lifetime I'll never lose her. Maybe one day soon we'll be able to move back into a relationship that won't horrify people. I hope so. Miriam and John would have been content being together, even if they had to live without sex, and there's no reason why Sally and I can't come to manifest that same depth of love.

CHAPTER 6

Irrational Obsessions

No matter how you try you just can't get on with your life because there's always a certain something preying on your mind. It might be a good thing or a bad thing, an obsessive hobby or fear, but either way it's blocking every thought process you have. You can't get the subject out of your mind, and you return to fuss or worry over it, every hour of the day.

You might be obsessed with a certain time or place in history, or you might be convinced that you're going to fall prey to a certain illness, or you might be an avid collector of things that aren't even aesthetically pleasing, and yet being surrounded with them makes you feel comfortable. It's irrational.

This kind of obsession can develop slowly, over years, or in some cases, it can be sudden, triggered by a visit to somewhere you were once connected to, or even by hearing a phrase that struck a chord within you. In the case of an obsession about a certain time or place, or the things associated with it, you're harking back to a past life when you were happier than you perceive yourself to be now. Collecting items from that period or place brings back some of the happiness you felt while living that life.

One of the most destructive kinds of obsessions is that of fear, perhaps of illness or even death. You're wasting your whole life worrying about it being over, yet still that moment is spoiled for you by the fear of it ending. In the case of a debilitating fearful obsession, it will be that there is a past life trauma you haven't accepted and healed, or a past life death that you experienced or witnessed, was so traumatic, it's all you can think about.

*

All I can ever think about is when I die

Georgina had a debilitating fear of death. It was something she thought about constantly and always knew it was going to be a horrible experience. Like anyone who has this fear, she ended up not enjoying her life at all, living in constant anticipation of it ending. I sent her to see the regressionist Stan Gerard.

Georgina: *I could see my husband, Sandy Craig, as he stood on the gallows, but I couldn't reach him. I so wanted to hold him in my arms and take him home, but as he stood crying in fear at what was about to happen to him, I was helpless. It was both a physical and emotional torment. My mind writhed in agony. I'd already watched two men hang that morning, and it was hard to imagine a more horrible death. They died choking and thrashing, the life cruelly squeezed out of them by the hangman's rope.* (No wonder I still feared death after seeing that!)

When it started

It had started in the year of 1857, in Drumcraig, in Ayrshire. I was called Susan Craig, and this particular day I was at home with our children Samuel and Jane and their father, Sandy. Sandy had earlier confessed to me that he had stolen some beasts from the Laird, Stuart, who lived in the castle nearby. He'd only done it to help feed his family, but I feared that now we'd lose him. Those worst fears were realized when the Laird and his men came to the house to arrest Sandy. He had hidden in the back, but when the men frightened me and the children, smashing up the house, threatening and manhandling us, he had no choice but to come out of hiding, and they pounced aggressively on him and took him away. We were all devastated, and I was so upset that I could barely give comfort to my young ones.

Later

I went to visit Sandy in prison, but he never wanted me to go there. He told me to go home and look to the bairns (children), and to forget all about him. But how could I? I could never forget about him, and no matter what he said or how much he protested, I had to follow him to his last breath.

Later

So, that was how I found myself in Peebles, watching men hang; hearing the crowds jeering and yelling out, "Murderer!" and waiting for it to be Sandy's turn to die. But my Sandy wasn't a murderer; he had only stolen another man's beasts, and he had only done that to try and provide for his family. How could that be a crime to be hanged for? I wanted to put a stop to it, my whole body cried out for me to save him, but I was powerless. It was the worst possible feeling.

Georgina: I was able to stand the regression right up to when they placed the noose around my husband's neck, and then I got so upset that Stan had to take me away from the sight. Knowing that the memories were bound to be traumatic, he'd previously established a 'safe place' in my mind – back when I was a child in this life, in 1972 in Torry, Aberdeen, and with a click of his fingers he moved me there.

This safe place is a place that I'm now able to retreat to whenever my fears start to bring on a panic attack, and so my life is much calmer now. I'm investigating all the things I saw, and the names, dates and places, and much to my amazement they're proving to be right. Knowing where my fear started is giving me a lot of power to control it.

Stan: Regression, simply, is an exercise in remembering. Our unconscious mind stores everything we have ever sensed. Regression back by a few days, or weeks, months, or years, in this life, can clarify facts and establish the cause of triggered fears or phobias. Past-life recall is simply a case of remembering from further down the 'memory stack'. Locating the fear and anxiety from past experiences, and achieving release of the fear, allows us to move-on, with therapeutic benefit, and far more confidence in ourselves – and in the future.

*

Witnessing a violent death in a past life, especially that of a loved-one, and the emotional scarring of not being able to do anything to help them, is a common theme in people who have this obsession with death. Interestingly, it doesn't happen quite so much when people have personally experienced a violent death themselves, although it can happen. The reason that your own violent death doesn't traumatize the soul quite as often, or as much, as witnessing that of a loved one, is that the soul or subconscious knows that physical death wasn't the end for it. Taking a person back through their own violent death and out the other side, can quickly erase feelings of dread of death. This is because they can plainly see that they have come back since that death, and so death for them is not the end, whereas terrible loss can seem like it's going to be forever, and so it's harder to heal. This is because although everyone will be reincarnated, and we may very well meet our loved ones again in their new bodies, they won't be exactly the same as they were before, and will most likely no longer be the much-loved parent, lover or child they once were. The thing to remember is that one day we *will* be reunited with them in their spirit form, and that however they appear, they will be the true essence of the person we have always known and loved.

*

I know this place
Jeffrey Keene's experiences are a classic case of spontaneous memory of past lives. When he was in the area of Maryland, in the

USA, he suddenly and inexplicably felt compelled to visit Antietam Battlefield Park, the scene of a Civil War battle. He felt compelled to go to the part known as *Sunken Lane*, and what happened there led him to an unshakable belief that in a past life he had been an American General.

This kind of unexpected experience, where your emotions run higher than normal, and remain embedded in you, so that even the memory of the incident brings a flood of emotional connections, are classic symptoms of past life flashbacks.

Jeffrey: *I walked down onto the road itself. I had only gone a few yards when something very strange happened, the likes of which I hope will never happen again. A wave of grief, sadness and anger washed over me. Without warning, I was suddenly being consumed by sensations. Burning tears ran down my cheeks. It became difficult to breathe. I gasped for air, as I stood transfixed in the old roadbed.*

To this day I could not tell you how much time transpired, but as these feelings, this emotional overload passed, I found myself exhausted as if I had run a marathon.

Crawling up the steep embankment to get out of the road, I turned and looked back.

I was a bit shaken to say the least and wondered at what had just taken place. It was difficult getting back to the car because I felt so weak. I had regained most of my normal composure on the way back and said nothing to Anna, my wife, about what had just happened. What could I say? How could I explain it to her? I did not have any answers, just questions. I would one day receive my answers, but not until more than a year later and then from a most unusual source.

Jeffrey found out later that he had walked into precise the location of the 6th Alabama, commanded by Col. John B. Gordon. Then when he saw General Gordon's picture in the *Civil War Quarterly* magazine he bought at Antietam, he recognized the face as his own.

Jeffrey: It was totally unnerving. Many people are startled by the resemblance when they view our pictures side by side. When I arrived home I checked the photos out. Ever since the time of being shot, Gordon was always photographed from the right side because of the deep scar under his left eye (the entry point of the bullet). Anyone who knows about bullet wounds knows that the damage becomes greater as a bullet travels through flesh, striking bone, expanding and fragmenting as it goes. The photo was a 3/4 view. One of the copies was an enlargement of Gordon's face. You could just make out the indentation under his left eye. You could see where the right side of his face had been blown out. There was an area from his right cheekbone down to his jaw and back to his ear that had seen better days.

Then something else caught my eye, it was a line that started at mid-ear and zigzagged across his cheek, almost like a lightning streak. I walked into the bathroom and stood before the mirror, photo in hand. On the right side of my face starting at mid-ear is a scar, light but discernible. It moves across my cheek in a zigzag pattern. Under my left eye there is an area about the size of a quarter, indented a little with a jagged line outlining most of it. I looked at the photo again and did a double take. The mark on the left side of my face was in the same place as the entry wound under Gordon's eye. I was not only receiving confirmation of a past life; I was being beaten over the head with it.

In the book *Someone Else's Yesterday*, Jeffrey Keene chronicles his journey as he relentlessly unravels the story of his past life as General John B Gordon. http://www.confederateyankee.net/

*

Imagination or Memory?

June Kydd was writing a fictional novel, or so she thought. She felt very inspired as she wrote, and believed this was due to her using the 'Silva Method' of meditation. She knew that this method was developed to increase the person's powers of intuition, but she still thought that her emotional story of a woman she called Ruth, was something her imagination was creating. She didn't have a clue why, but she was compelled to call the book, *Unshriven*.

The book was set in 1963, but another storyline, which didn't seem to fit into the book invaded June's mind, and would not be shaken off. It involved a woman called Hannah Miller, and the injustice that befell her in August 1663. Hannah died, condemned for a wrong she did not commit.

Compelled to acknowledge Hannah's life, eventually June decided to incorporate that story within the book as a past life memory of Ruth's. June 'invented' a home for Hannah in a terrace of 300-year-old cottages set in a fictitious hamlet near Stratford-on-Avon. Less than a month later she found herself, quite coincidentally, in the cottage by the shallow ford where she had placed what she had thought was a fictional character, in the very hamlet that she thought she had invented.

*

June: I went on to discover the reality of the 1663 episodes – what I had thought was a work of fiction. I was aware of everything around me in unbelievable detail: a fireplace hidden behind a false wall, another with a hearth-stone and bread oven (big enough to hide a small child), part of a previous dwelling on the site, two steps leading up to a blank wall in the attic, and the exact spot of an underground spring in the garden where, according to my spiritual information, someone had once been hastily buried.

I visited the Manor house where Hannah had lived in the two

attic rooms overlooking the remains of an abandoned village. There are no historic records of the village, but apparently the year before the outlines had been visible, and photographed from the air during a severe drought. In the little churchyard, (once linked to the Manor by an underground passage), its peripheral decoration still sharp, was a 17th Century headstone that held no name. It marked the grave of a woman who had died unshriven.

All this and more was exactly as I had written months before I ever visited the place.

Hannah Miller's spirit is tied to this earth by a wicked miscarriage of justice. Her ghost is still seen on the stairs of the Manor house, and her message is this, "I will not rest until the truth of this injustice is told, and the shame lifted from my family name."

*

Years ago, the worst possible thing that people believed could happen to a person was to die unshriven – to die with their sins still not forgiven. Hannah has come back as June, in this lifetime, to help her to put right that wrong, and this is a prime example of someone awakening to their master plan – the overriding reason they have come back here.

CHAPTER 7

Lack of Self-Worth and Self-Harming

No matter how you try, you just don't feel as if you or your life is worth anything. No matter how much someone might say they love you, it doesn't make any difference, you still feel the same about yourself. If you feel very bad you might even take to harming yourself, and for a while that makes you feel better in your mind, as if you deserved to be punished. This harming can take many forms, from overindulging with food or drink or drugs, to more physically manifested punishment, such as cutting or burning your own skin. It could be that you stay in an abusive or violent relationship, because that's all you think you deserve. Or you might develop an eating disorder, such as anorexia or bulimia. You want it to stop, but you are the one doing it, and you have no control over yourself.

I'm Innocent

Jemma had this problem. She felt so miserable all of the time, and could see no point to her life. The only time she ever felt any better about herself was for the few brief hours after she had made some new elaborate cuts on her forearms, to join the healed over scars from the last times. She felt very guilty all the time, but she had never done anything wrong in this lifetime. She had not been abused as a child and there seemed to be no reason for her to hate herself the way she manifestly did.

This was a case where the regression had to be handed very carefully indeed, to avoid making the situation worse.

Jemma: *The girl is screaming, but I have to shut my ears. They push the* stool under the water again and she plunges down into the murky pond water. I think this will be the last time. She's going to be proven innocent, and so she must die. It's so wrong. My name is Jeremy Planton and I am employed by a witch finder. It's 1647 and I'm in East Anglia under the employment of John Stearne. When he took me on I was glad enough of the work. He took me, starving from the gutter, and for some time I felt I was entitled to fight to survive, but after a while, all the young women, dying, at my hand, for nothing, started to destroy me as surely as starvation would have done. Hardly any were proved guilty, so innocents were the ones I was killing. Today is no exception, and to make matters worse, the girl's mother is on her knees, pleading with me to stop it. There is nothing I can do, the way the law stands, if they're accused, they have to be tried. If they don't drown, then I have to kill them anyway.

I can see another woman, standing out in the crowd, and judging by her smug face she probably engineered this accusation for her own ends. Most probably she coveted the accused woman's husband. He is nowhere to be seen, so he should feel ashamed, accusing his own wife of making her children sick with devilment.

The girl is brought up, Mary Graham is her name, was her name. She is limp, dead, drowned, for nothing but an unfaithful husband and his trollop.

Later

I have tried to break away from this terrible life, but to no avail. I was told that if I rescinded my authority I would stand accused myself. Maybe that would be better, but I'm not strong enough. Though shamed with every breath of my body, I continue to work for the witch finder, and more innocents die by my hand. I am no better than a murderer.

Later

I have a fever. I'm about to leave the world and I'm glad. I swear I have learned and I hope that if there is a next life I will be forgiven.

Well of course Jemma *had* been forgiven, by the universe, by her angels, but not by herself. She still felt a continuous need to give Jeremy the punishment he had wanted to give himself.

I spent some time counseling her after the session, gradually healing the pain she felt, and taking her through two other lives she'd had between the one as Jeremy and the one as Jemma. In those lives she had rediscovered and then helped most of those whom she'd wronged in the 1600s lifetime. But when she came through this time, as had happened in other lives, all she felt was the guilt from her time as a witch finder.

I explained to her that at least as Jeremy she had started to wake up to the wrong he was doing and to the possibility, on his deathbed, of making up for that wrong.

I took her briefly through several other lives to demonstrate the point that he did make amends in the end. Eventually, once she had the whole picture, she was able to reconcile how she felt about herself. In this life she can only be Jemma, and Jemma is a sweet and kind person who should not be punished.

I believe she will stop cutting herself now. In cases like this one has to very carefully build the whole jigsaw, before the client is able to see their whole picture. Just seeing a fragment is quite often not enough.

Jemma: At last I understand why I feel the way I do. I understand why I felt like a bad person even though I've done nothing wrong in this life. I'm going to forgive Jeremy now. He was a misguided soul who suffered a lot himself, and repented, or tried to, and then tried to make up for what he'd done.

I am not Jeremy, I am Jemma, and from today I plan to only be me!

*

I'm worth it

Paul was another story. He too was a self-harmer, and yet it didn't seem to come from a feeling of guilt. He would flinch if anyone shouted at him or moved suddenly. He had all the signs of someone who had been abused as a child, which often later leads to self-abuse, and yet he assured me that he had not been abused in this lifetime.

He was also unable to say 'No' to anything, and was so humble and self-effacing that it was hard to believe he'd been brought up in a normal, functional and loving family, as he had been. We had to go back a lot further than his current lifetime in order to discover where the roots of his feelings came from.

Paul: *I'm being dragged. I'm only a small boy, about ten years old, and they're dragging me. Soldiers in uniform are dragging me away. I won't walk, I won't go on there. I can't stop them. They're pushing me through the door, and now I'm in there…Help me!*

At this point Paul became so distressed that he could barely breathe, so we had to go back further to a slightly less terrifying time. He couldn't remember everything that happened to him after he'd been dragged into that room, and it was right that he shouldn't do so. He had been a Romani boy, who was taken to a concentration camp and experimented on. These feelings he had of lack of worth were generated in that time, when he had been treated with less respect and regard than the most pitiful laboratory rat. It had been ingrained into him that his life, his feelings, his emotions, his pain and his needs, were of no importance whatsoever. His death in that life was a release in the end from unimaginable torture and torment. That feeling of knowing one is going to die, being mutilated and maimed so that the end is inevitable and yet won't come quickly enough to relieve the suffering, is damaging in the extreme.

It took a long time to heal that life for Paul. Many times he had to do a releasing meditation in order to detach, finally, from that dreadful life. He also thought that he must have previously been a bad soul to have suffered so much in that lifetime. This wasn't the case, but even if it had been discovered that he had meted out abuse to someone else in a previous lifetime that would have no bearing on the more evolved soul of today, and punishment is not appropriate.

It will take a lot more counseling for Paul to become truly confident, but at least he now has the knowledge he needs to start on the road to recovery, and he has stopped abusing himself. He was only doing that to avoid facing what his subconscious knew deep down. In his regression, unlike in the usual ones, he actually needed help to forget, rather than to remember. He needed a basic knowledge of what was done, and who was to blame (ie not himself) but then he needed a strategy with which to put Pandora back in the box.

Paul: It was traumatic to go back to that body, but it was worth it. Now I know that I felt unworthy just because I was told I was, and treated as if I was, and not because I *was* unworthy. I've managed to detach from that life now, and forgive all the people who did that to me. I think I'll eventually be able to drop all that baggage and get on with this life, which I now believe will be good. I haven't had to abuse my body for over six months now, so I believe that chapter of my life is over.

Paul: I'm going into counseling to help others who self-harm, and I can't help but wonder how many of their problems will be down to past life traumas.

This opens up a whole new avenue for treating people with this problem, and I'm very excited at the thought of being a part of it. I feel this is what I came here for, and knowing my master plan has given me great passion for what I'm doing. That in turn is boosting my self-confidence, and filling me with a sense of being important in the world. I have never felt this happy before in all my life.

*

There are many other causes for a lack of confidence and self-worth. One woman who wrote to me had a lot of spiritual knowledge and had been practicing Wicca for a while, but she was very nervous of people, and expected them to make fun of her.

Her past life angel had given her an early nudge towards her past, which meant it was very important for her to have it healed. She had a wonderful pathway to walk in this lifetime, and to remember what it was, she needed to remember who she really was. She was once a court jester, and people *did* laugh at her, but only because she wanted them to – her life depended on it. Despite the laughter, jesters were actually extremely quick-witted and intelligent – they really had to be. Making a grumpy king laugh, or not, could mean the difference between keeping your head or losing it! There is more to this woman than meets the eye, and now that her past has been healed, people will know it one day.

*

A young boy of ten years old wrote to me. He said, "I have a large brown birthmark on my tummy. I'm very anxious about it and I don't like swimming lessons because people stare at it and ask what it is. Might it have been caused by something I can be proud of instead?"

After getting permission from his mother I was able to reveal that in 1830 he was a Comanche boy, who was sent on his first buffalo hunt when he was thirteen. His horse fell down, and the boy was gored in the stomach by a male buffalo. Despite this, he still managed to spear the buffalo and kill it. He recovered from the wound and was esteemed because of the bravery he'd showed. He became initiated as a warrior, aged only fourteen, a year earlier than normal, and was eventually elected as a war chief, an honor only given to the most respected men. He was called Buffalo Hump (Po-cha-na-quar-hip), and he was a very brave warrior.

Following this revelation the young man's mother was able to report that things changed dramatically and her son enjoyed amazing people who stared at his tummy, with the story of where the mark came from.

*

Another woman wrote to me because she said, "Please tell me who I am and why I feel I don't belong. Sometimes I can just sit in the cinema and cry because I feel lost. All my life I have felt this way and I really need a helping hand. I don't know who else to turn to. Please help me find myself and some confidence."

She felt like she didn't belong because she yearned to go back to a particularly wonderful past life. In 1280 she lived in the palace of Dadu in China.

Her life today seems so dull and lacking in grandeur compared to the one she enjoyed then. Without the importance of her position in that life, her current life felt worthless. The city is known today as Beijing, and her master plan in this life is to revisit it.

Now that she knows where she'll feel a sense of belonging, doors will open to enable her to reach her goal, even if she couldn't see a path there right now. Once she has done that, this current life will open to her and she'll find her soul's home.

CHAPTER 8

Phobias

This chapter is longer than any other in this book. That's because its subject, phobias, is by far and away the most common symptom of a past life that needs resolution. More than half of the letters and emails I get are asking me about help for phobias.

You feel really silly and yet there's nothing you can do about it. Every time you see a particular *something* that the rest of the population considers completely harmless, it sends you into a shaky-legged, spiral of sheer panic. In your case it could be cotton wool, a sparrow, a button, or almost anything. You have a phobia.

You've questioned parents and family, and no one can shed any light on the situation. Nothing has ever scared you enough to cause the phobia, for as far back as anyone can remember. Why on earth would someone be scared by a blob of cotton wool anyway?

The reason no one can remember the incident is because this will be back further than anyone *can* remember, without some help, that is.

I've seen the most bizarre phobias cured at a stroke, by the actual event that triggered it being revealed, analyzed, and healed. Knowledge, in this case, really is power. Knowing why a cat, for instance, terrifies you, just by being next to you on the pavement is at least halfway towards conquering that fear with logic. Making sense of these nonsensical fears can stop them in their tracks.

Imagine you did have a phobia of shiny brass buttons. People might suggest to you that perhaps you once died by choking on such a button. This is possible. However, that would more likely cause a phobia of coughing or choking. One case of a fear of buttons I came across turned out to have quite a different origin.

The woman in question was once a man, who was throttled by an army soldier, who had shiny brass buttons in two rows down the front of his tunic. These buttons were the last thing the man saw, right in front of his eyes, as his life ebbed away. His psyche had come to associate the buttons with his fear and trauma, rather than the soldier behind them.

Imagine being scared of ducks. They in themselves are pretty harmless, but imagine if you were once a young child who drowned in a farm pond. Perhaps the last time you reached the surface before dying, you startled the farm ducks that were swimming on the pond, and the last thing you associated with your death was them quacking and flapping around your face. You could come to fear the ducks rather than drowning.

One man I knew was terrified of seagulls. At first he just stayed away from the coast to avoid them, but of course nowadays gulls are pretty much everywhere, so life was very difficult for him. It turned out that he had once belonged to a tribe who ate sea-gull eggs as part of their staple diet. He had been climbing the cliffs collecting eggs from nests, when a gull suddenly flew in his face, and the shock of the attack made him let go of the rocks and plummet to his death on the shore below. The fear of seagulls stayed with him long after he fell to his death.

So, you can see that it's not always an actual object that did you harm that comes through as a phobia, but it can be an object that you associate with a subsequent frightening death, during the last moments of which you saw that particular object.

Of course, sometimes you have phobias of more logical things that can be in some way inherently dangerous, such as flying, but unless there is a reason for it to have grown from normal commonsense anxiety into full-blown, disempowering terror, which cannot be talked or medicated away, the chances are its origins are in your distant past.

*

Inanimate Objects

Katrina wrote to me because a phobia was blighting her life. Her fear was of white statues. Nothing in her childhood could explain it and no amount of conventional therapy could cure it. The phobia had started at the age of five, and as she had grown up, it had got steadily worse. When she was younger, other children thought it was funny to torment her on school trips, once pushing her headlong into a statue of a horse. She hyperventilated with terror and almost passed out, so great was the trauma inflicted on her by an inanimate, concrete object.

Soon she had to avoid going anywhere that had white statues. Then in 2003 she and her husband went to York Minster, and she had a terrible incident there. She found herself sweating and 'crying like a baby', after coming face to face with a statue at the entrance. She'd curled up in a ball on the ground, her arms clutching an unseen object to her chest. Quite a crowd of solicitous strangers gathered around trying to help. She was mortified and embarrassed and decided she had to face her fear at last and find out the root cause of it.

I sent her to see Janet Thompson.

Katrina: *I'm inside a small, dark building. I know it's my home, and I know the house is in Rome some centuries ago. I live there with my mother and baby son. I work in a big place that has a lot of columns and big statues.* (Janet later said that I shuddered at the thought.) *The people there are rich and they made unkind and hard masters. I have to take my tiny son to my work with me every day, because there's no one else to look after my baby. My mother is too old and sick to take care of him, and I have to work to feed us all.*

Later

Suddenly, I'm filled with terror. I'm at my place of work and the ground is moving. Big holes and cracks are opening all around me. I struggle to stay on my feet, screaming with fear. I try to cover my baby's face as I desperately search for a way out, amid the swirling, choking clouds of dust that fill the air. I hear the sounds of stone crashing to the ground, and shards cut into me. I look up and see with horror that a massive statue of a horse and rider is toppling over onto me. There's a sudden, shocking impact, and everything goes dark. I cry out, "It killed me! Where's my baby? My baby!"

Janet tries to soothe me, "Just let your spirit leave that body and hover around, and look down from above. Look down without fear and just observe the details. Tell me what you can see. Can you see your body?"

I can just see my feet and one of my arms sticking out from underneath the rubble. I can't see my baby.

Janet says, "Just let yourself look to the side of you and see the spirit of your baby."

Suddenly I can feel him back in my arms. I sob with relief and hold him tightly, knowing that we're together in spirit.

Janet reassures me, "So he's quite safe now. You are both quite safe now. When you are ready just let your spirit leave that lifetime and all that belongs in the past. Let you and your baby ascend into the light.

Janet: Katrina then went into the light and met with her soul group and her primary spirit guide. I asked her to request some understanding of that life and the karmic connections with this life. Her guide told her that she needed to go and touch a white statue and then she would know that her fear was gone.

Katrina: I couldn't believe how uplifted I felt. That very day I was able to walk into a shop and look through a book on sculptures, for the first time in this life, without panicking. I then went to a garden centre and am now planning a trip to the British Museum and then St Paul's Cathedral.

For Janet, having her baby torn from her arms and seeing him dead beneath the rubble, was far more traumatic to Katrina that her own death at the same time.

This emotional scarring, generated by her inability to save him, brought through an exaggerated fear of the instrument of his death – a statue.

Logic told her after her regression that it wasn't in fact the statue that had killed him – it was inanimate. It was the earthquake that had caused the statue to fall that was to blame for her baby's death. A fear of earthquakes, which is all she is now left with, is a reasonably logical and normal one. And she knows that as long as she stays out of earthquake regions, she no longer needs to fear statues.

*

Masking fear

A woman called Yvonne wrote to me because she had a great fear of masks and headdresses that covered more than the eyes, and also she had a great affinity with the county of Norfolk, which she describes as her 'spiritual home'.

She also lived with a dread of storms, which was so bad that it was almost taking over her life. Just one dark cloud on the horizon was enough to trigger a panic attack.

I sent her to see the regressionist Moira Fitzsimmonds.

Yvonne: *It's 1413 AD. My name is Emily, and I'm 17 years old. I live in Norfolk by the sea. I love it here – it's just lovely. I feel so happy. (I* could feel my face brighten up at the mere thought of the place.) *My family doesn't live here – I am alone. I work at the local inn, serving beer to the local men. I love working here. I don't go far though, I feel safe here. I love walking by the sea – it's my favourite place to be, in my small world.*

Later

I am transported in time to my wedding day – I don't know the year. I don't understand that type of thing. Dates mean nothing to me. I'm 21 years old, and wearing flowers in my hair. My husband John is so kind, but I know that he is not going to live very long. (When I looked into John's eyes, I knew he was now my husband, Andrew, from this life!) *He works in the fields digging, and we are very happy. I knew this was to be short lived.*

Later

He's gone away. He's out on a ship, and there's a terrible storm. The ship's sinking. He manages to escape, but he is so unwell that he dies after a short time. He was only young – 25 years old I think. He's left me alone with our daughter Anne. We feel so sad. I am too young to be on my own.

Later

Now I'm only 30 years old – sitting by and watching the sea – it's lovely – the most special place in the world.

Another Lifetime

It's 1666 AD. I am seven years old and I live in Whitechapel, London. I am so little, I've got long straggly hair, and my clothes are dirty, and I'm wearing thin shoes. I am terrified, and feel so distressed. I am stuck in a small room on my own – I cannot go anywhere. I spend my days looking out of the small window – all I can see are the men wearing their long black cloaks, and they wear masks. Black masks that look like a long bird's beak. *They are horrible. Those men in masks are like devils to me. I am terrified that they are going to come in and take me to the place where they keep the dead bodies. Every day and night they walk around looking for the dead. But I am alive! I have not got the plague. Why have they left me here alone? My family has all died – the men have taken them away from me. I am just here, waiting to die.*

Later
It was too late by the time they came looking for me. I died. I was so scared – I died of sadness. The last thing I saw before I lost consciousness was those masks as the men wearing them came to take me.

Moira: Yvonne's fear of masks surfaced, and also her fear of storms. Her beloved husband was taken from her because of one. As to her having an affinity with Norfolk, is it any wonder? It was her happiest life, and her husband now was her husband then. In all of the lives explored she loved being by the sea.

Since the session, I've had an email from Yvonne. She has noticed subtle differences in her life, as has her husband. She is more positive and her fears are almost like they belong to someone else. She has become more of an observer in her phobias and fears, rather than a participant. I feel a new chapter in her life is about to begin.

Yvonne: My husband and I visited a tiny place in Norfolk called Heacham, quite by chance a few years ago. We immediately fell in love with the place. It is so familiar to us. We're meant to be there, and when it came time to leave I didn't want to go.

I've been terrified of masks ever since I can remember – ones that cover the whole face in particular. Whether they are on television or in a book I cannot bear to look at them. I've always had a fascination with this period in history though. I know that the plague was rife in London in 1666. The thing that scared me most about the era was the plague masks they used to wear, and the strange thing is that when I used Jenny's Past Life CD a little while ago, I had exactly the same flashback of this previous lifetime.

Now that she knows where her fear of masks came from, Yvonne can rationalize it. She knows that should there ever be a dreadful epidemic in her current life, victims will be cared for in hospitals. She also knows that it wasn't the masks that killed her, but the disease, so she understands now that masks themselves cannot harm her.

It's logical to be aware of the possibilities of infection from diseases, but not to be incapacitated by it.

*

Logical, but Out of Control Fears

Biting terror

I got a heart-rending letter from Chanté, telling me that her honeymoon in the south of France was going to be ruined because of her fear of sharks. She couldn't even look at a cartoon shark. She was certainly not going to be able to enjoy a dip with her new hubby, even in the hotel pool, because despite logically knowing that it would be impossible to come across a shark in a pool, she knew from previous experience that as soon as she was immersed in the water, her fear would make her panic. A concern about sharks in some waters in sensible, but not in a swimming pool. She desperately needed help and fast, so I sent her to see Moira Fitzsimmons, near Birmingham.

Chanté: *I see an old, wooden, blue door dated 1726. As I go through I become a 40-year-old woman, wearing heavy woolen dresses in lots of layers. I can see the sea, and a port with white buildings. It's Bristol. I'm on the dock with the crew, who are loading boxes and barrels onto a ship.*

Later

I'm in the galley (ship's kitchen). The ship is swaying from side-to-side and things are rolling about the room and smashing. I can hear shouting and running from on deck. I climb the stairs onto the deck, barely able to keep my feet, and stand near the back of the boat. A huge storm is raging and the boat is being shaken badly. Huge waves are crashing over the edges. People are shouting and very frightened, as I cling tightly to a rail. A fight starts as people are trying to get help to escape, but then there's a loud bang from below, and the ship starts to tip over. I see some of the crew fall overboard. I cling to the side of the ship, but my feet keep slipping. The ship starts to sink and I can't hold on anymore. We're too far from land to be rescued and also I can't swim. As I fall in the water I start to panic. The noise of screaming, and the ship is all around me, whirling above my head. I keep going under the water but there's nothing to cling to. I see the terrifying shape of a shark coming toward me. I have no breath to scream as the water pours into my mouth. The shark bites into my left foot and lower leg. By now, I know I'm drowning, and I feel my spirit leave my body. I look down and see my body, and the shark, but feel calm. My left leg is tingling.

*

Moira: Chanté's regression was very vivid to her. She had a real fear of swimming in the sea and of sharks and in the regression she observed herself being eaten by sharks. I have since heard from her, and she now feels she will be able to swim in the sea on her honeymoon, and with time her shark phobia will subside completely. She feels it was a very positive experience.

Chanté: After the reading I felt relaxed. Moira said she'd seen my spirit guide join me, a male Aztec, who was a sort of priest or psychic. I already knew that my guide was a Mayan or possibly

Aztec priest, as I'd seen him in meditation, wearing a gold headdress like the sun, long white robes with a gold decoration and various colours in his robes. I call him Rainbow. It was really interesting that Moira saw him too.

I will definitely be able to swim in the sea now. After the regression the TV showed a brief clip of an overhead view of a shark swimming across the screen, and I didn't have a panic attack, though I did get butterflies in my stomach. I managed to look at cartoon pictures of sharks, just feeling a little sick in the tummy. Both these things are massive achievements for me. I wish to thank everyone involved with making this possible.

In Chanté's case seemed it was her own death that created the phobia. But really it was her terror and anticipation leading up to the attack that caused the trauma to come through to this life. It was this fear that Moira had to heal, because it was the terror she felt before the attack that caused her to panic whenever she was in water of any kind. The feel of the water on her legs, gave her spontaneous flashbacks to that time of fear. I heard from Chanté later, and she told me that her honeymoon went without a hitch. She was able to swim in the pool with her new husband, and felt that she would soon be able to swim in the sea too.

*

Premonition or Past Event?

Jane had a debilitating fear that she was going to be attacked. Sometimes past events come to us in visions or dreams that are so strong, we think we're seeing events yet to come. Jane had got to the point where she could only sleep if she hid a big knife under her pillow. Her partner, naturally, was a bit concerned about a knife-wielding, fearful person sleeping next to him, so I sent Jane to see therapist, Sue Tribe.

Jane: *The year is 1742. I'm wearing flat shoes made of some white material, and have on a cream dress, which feels soft on my skin. I am 24 years old and my name is Rebecca. I live in Wiltshire, England, with my parents. My father is wealthy and he works with lots of papers and documents. We have maids at home. I can clearly see my bedroom, with a dressing table, and a jewelry box on it, a hairbrush, comb and mirror.*

Later
Father and I are traveling back from London in a carriage. It is dark and raining. I am scared because of the dark, and look out of the windows, fearfully. Suddenly the carriage stops and three men drag my father and me out.

(I started getting distressed at this point, wringing my hands, and Janet said later that my body was tensing).

They're hurting my father and holding me. They're beating father. I'm being held, standing up. (I became more distressed, crying and shaking, holding my body rigid).

My father is conscious, but not saying anything, his eyes are blank reflections. The men throw me to the ground and rape me, with my father watching. The men then kill my father, slitting his throat, and then they slit my throat.

Past the Moment of Death
Sue asked me where I could feel distress in my body, and I told her it was in my chest. She gave me a cushion to push against and told me I could fight the men off. I pushed them away. Sue asked where my emotional centre was, and I told her my stomach. I said that I had wanted my father to stop them to help me. I felt he should have saved me. I cried out, "Help me!" Sue asked what my father was saying, and I could hear his voice, asking me to forgive him. He said he would have stopped them if he could. It

tore him apart to watch me being raped. He was sorry. The feeling in my stomach went. Sue asked me if I wanted to say anything to the men who raped and murdered me. I said, "I hate them, they destroyed me. I don't want to see them."

Sue: It's wonderful that Jane can now start to live without the fear she has always had. She now recognizes it was a traumatic past life memory, and this will enable her to embrace the future in a more positive manner. Whilst there will be personal and private reflections for her about the impact of this work, Jane has recognized that she has sought to protect herself by having people in her life that will and can protect her, and this resonates with her feeling unprotected by her father in her past life.

Jane says: It helped me tremendously. I felt a bit strange for a couple of days after the session, and then one evening my hubby was watching a scary movie that would normally have made me frightened, but I went to bed on my own. It wasn't until I was in bed that I realized what I'd done. Also I've found myself not remembering if the doors are locked during the day, and even deliberately leaving the back door wide open when it was warm – which is unheard of for me.

*

In Jane's case it was her rage, helplessness, and sense of injustice that caused the trauma, more than the actual death itself. Rape victims can often bring through this sense of foreboding, which isn't about their actual death. Jane's anger at her father and her deep disappointment in what she saw as his unwillingness to save her was what caused her dread in this life. This was why she even felt a need to have a weapon when her husband was in bed with her. She couldn't let herself rely on him. Now that she knew that her father had been as helpless as she was, she could get hold of her fear and rationalize it. She knows that her husband will protect her in this life, and so her sense of needing to do it for herself has diminished.

CHAPTER 9

Claustrophobia and Agoraphobia

Everyone else in the elevator looks calm and unconcerned, but your palms are sweating and your pulse is racing. You don't understand why no one else seems to notice that the air's getting stuffy, the light seems to be failing, and the tin box you're standing in is getting smaller and more crowded by the second. You know that if the electricity fails and the light goes out completely, you'll start screaming or pass out. This is what it always feels like for you to be trapped in a small place. So whenever you can you take the stairs and avoid any confined spaces like the plague.

You're in a seaside town, and everyone else in your group is enjoying the walk through the caves, interconnected by tunnels that only just clear your head. In each cave room the others sit and watch and listen to the moving display, while your heart is starting to race, and the caves roof is starting to come down on you in your mind. Suddenly, panic takes over and like a hunted animal, unable to think or vocalize your terror; you start to run, literally bouncing off the walls, only knowing that you have to get out. As you run the tunnel walls get lower and lower and you know that if you don't find an exit soon you'll start screaming.

Or, maybe it all started years ago with a small feeling of anxiety every time you left the house. Just stepping over the threshold was enough to make you jittery. Gradually the fear increased and your world shrank. First, you stopped being able to walk anywhere outdoors, trips to the shops had to be done in a car with you only nipping out into the air for the time it took for you to reach the 'safety' of the shop doorway. Now you find it hard to leave the house at all. Even standing in a big room makes you feel nervy and tense. You like cozy corners, and slink around the edges of rooms, avoiding the open centre, but you have no idea what it is you're scared of.

Total Darkness

David was ashamed on his fears. It made his working life very difficult, because he often had to attend city meetings in high-rise office blocks. It was embarrassing for him to have to insist on climbing flights and flights of stairs and arrive to meetings breathless and disheveled, or risk going up in the elevator and perhaps emerge as a gibbering wreck, having blown all chances of promotion. He needed to get to the bottom of his problem.

David: *My name is Badru. I'm terrified, but I must act brave, or I'll be put to death in some horrifying way. I'm being locked in a tomb with two equally terrified women. Since the Pharaoh's death, I've known I might be chosen to accompany him on his voyage to the afterlife, but I hoped I'd be spared. I'm being dressed ready now, and baskets of provisions are being brought for the master's journey. I've managed to hide some forbidden items in the baskets and I pray they won't be discovered.*

Later

I'm inside the tomb. Two women, Nuru and Pili are in here with me. They've been drugged to make them calm, but I cheated and didn't drink the draught. The moment has come and the slab is being dragged into place above our heads. The women sit quietly, only their flashing eyes betraying their fear. The slab makes a horrendous noise, its weight grinding along and proving to us that we'd never be able to escape through it. There's a resounding clang and it drops into its slots. The light is cut off as if with a knife. The darkness is complete and we can't see anything, not even each other, though we're huddled closely together. The sunless cold starts to bite into our bones right away.

Later

Thank the Gods that my secrets are still safe. I have two torches and the means to light them. We were forbidden to bring light with us. It's wonderful to see the light, but it makes our predicament more real. We will die, there's no doubt. There's food and water, and a slow, suffocating death in the dark once the torches have gone out through lack of air. The tomb seems much smaller in the torchlight, and the wavering shadows make the walls seem to close in on us. My other package is also safe.

(David thought this package was probably arsenic). *I have brought enough poison for all of us. We'll take it. We were dead anyway the moment the tomb slab was closed, and at least this poison will spare us lingering.*

It wasn't just the dark and fear of death that made this memory have such impact on David's life; it was also the helplessness and the fear evident in the faces of the other people. The good thing about this memory was that David could see that as Badru, he had actually been very brave and had taken steps to lessen the ordeal of the two women he was shut in with. This boost to his self image would be a great help to him in his current life.

David: At last I have an answer, and something I can work with. I am going to develop a meditation of my own, following Jenny's instructions. I'll create a place of light and openness inside my heart and go there if I feel I can't control my fear. I'll practice first, going into dark and confined places and understanding that I'm no longer in that old situation in the tomb, that I'm not going to die in there, and I will soon be out in the light again.

*

Surrounded By Danger

Denise had the opposite problem. She could have happily lived in an elevator. She loved visiting caves and her own living room was stuffed so full of furniture that it was hard to move around. This was because Denise had gradually got to the state where she didn't even like being in an empty or spacious room. It had started off with her feeling anxious about going outside, but it had become much, much worse than that. Now she didn't even feel safe inside her own home, unless she could always be touching some item of furniture, or walk around the room hugging the walls.

This was all because she hadn't woken up with that first nudge from her past life angel. Things had become more severe as she refused to understand what the message meant. The only way to solve her problem was to take her back to when it really began, which was not in this lifetime.

Denise: *I'm warm, wrapped up safe and snug. I'm just a toddler, but I understand that I live in a hot, humid country. I think it must be India. I'm a little girl, called Shadri. I can hear my parents arguing. I don't really understand what they're saying, but my mother is very upset and crying. She keeps hugging me and crying. My father pushes a small pouch into my mother's hand and turns and runs from the room. My mother, still crying, puts me down and mixes some powder from the pouch with water. She starts to give it to me to drink. It tastes nasty, bitter, and I spit it out. My mother sobs even more. She grabs me up and takes me outside.*

Later
We're out on the empty sands. My mother puts me on the rocky ground and places a water skin in my hands. She drops a basket full of fruit at my feet, and then she turns and walks quickly away. I start to cry and call after her. I get up in a wobbly way and try to run after her. But I can't keep up. I'm crying and staggering and I can't see for tears.

Later

I must have fallen down and cried myself to sleep. Now I'm awake and it's almost dark. There are many stars and a full moon in the sky, so I can see for miles. But all I can see is nothing and no one. I don't remember which direction my mother went in, and I don't remember where the water skin is. I'm thirsty and hungry. I call out and call out until my voice breaks and I can't call any more. My eyes are on stalks as I look and look for someone to help me. There is no one, just emptiness, and I'm cold.

Later

It's morning. No one has come. I can't see any shelter or any life. I crawl up a rock and from the top I can see further. There's nothing as far as I can see. I cry.

*

It became obvious that Shadri's mother had been ordered to poison her by her family. She couldn't do it, so instead chose to abandon her baby in the desert. Shadri probably had some defect, such as a hair-lip, and that coupled with her being a girl, meant she had no future in the culture of the time, and would drag her family down. Maybe Shadri's mother thought she was being merciful, and really thought she was giving her daughter some sort of chance, whereas in fact she was condemning her to a lonely and slow death. To Shadri, the real horror was that after living in a crowded village, she was suddenly cast into a void. Fear of being in a void had come through with her. Now that she understands where her fear started, and that she is no longer in that kind of danger, Denise will be able to open up her life to the world again.

Denise: What a horrible way to die, but more horrible was that feeling of fear and abandonment and wanting desperately to see some signs of life. The space around me felt cold and dangerous, which is how I've come to feel about my own living room.

Bringing my fears out into the cold light of day has made me see clearly that they're not relevant to my current life.

Now I'm ready to do some clearing the clutter. I'm going to make my home my own again, every corner of it, and I'm certain that I'll be able to start going out again.

I did a healing the inner child exercise with Jenny, and brought poor little Shadri back into the safety of my soul. This works by you visualizing the child, and her plight, but as an adult, as you are now. You can then see how you might have been able to help the child, if you'd been there. Then you absorb the child into your current body, nurturing her and healing her pain. From now on, I'll be the adult protecting her, so she won't be afraid anymore, and neither will I.

*

Claustrophobia can also manifest as a fear of crowds. One woman wrote to me saying, "When I'm in a crowd, I panic. In crowded venues I have to have an aisle seat to stop myself from getting edgy. Perhaps if you could tell me why. Then my friends, who think I'm strange, might be more understanding."

It turned out that when she read the news in 1989 about how Hillsborough suffered the tragedy of 86 people dying from being crushed when a football stadium collapsed, it triggered her own memories when 33 people died the same way when some barriers collapsed in the Bolton Wanderer's ground in 1946. Too many people had been admitted to the match against Stoke City. When the barriers collapsed under weight of numbers, the crowd from those stands fell onto her, and many others, causing them to be asphyxiated and crushed. No wonder she's having panic attacks in crowds today. Now her friends will understand that having been through the terror of being squashed underfoot, she must sit where she feels safe without ridicule. However, now that she knows why she has the fear, it will diminish.

*

Another woman suffering from agoraphobia wrote to me complaining that she couldn't make any decisions. She would stand on her doorstep every morning, unable to decide whether she felt able to venture outside. This lack of decisiveness gradually grew until she was unable to go outside at all, even if she wanted to. She had twin babies, so life was impossible and every new responsibility only made her feel worse.

She was learning some tough lessons. In her past life she had opted out, becoming a nun, living in a protected and controlled environment, and just doing what she was told. Now she was having to learn to make her own decisions, and stand up for herself she was being overwhelmed with responsibility. She also needed to tell her twin's father and her siblings that they must help her more. She needed to willingly grasp the purpose of the lessons, which was that she needed to value herself more. She needed to feel she was capable of an independent life and her future would slowly but surely get better.

*

Another interesting case of agoraphobia said, "For 17 years I've suffered from bad panic attacks. I've been agoraphobic for 12 years and find it very hard to leave home. Please can you help me? I want my life back.

It transpired that in 1843, aged just nine, she was sent to work as a maidservant. The barbaric punishment meted out to her when she couldn't do all the heavy work required of her, was to shut her in the coal hole. This cellar would have been as black as night when the hatches were shut. Although she actually suffered from a fear of open spaces, as a child the stygian black would have seemed like an infinite and bottomless void, possibly inhabited by all kinds of monsters, hence her fear of open spaces.

She needed to create a safe place deep in her soul, furnish it with everything she loves, and retreat there in her mind when she feels the panic rising, knowing she is totally safe. Healing can take a little while when the trauma is deep seated, but knowledge of why she has the fear will soon start to lessen it.

CHAPTER 10

Spontaneous Flashbacks – am I going mad?

You literally feel out of place, to the extent that you're almost living a double life. You don't seem to fit in your current era, and you're uncomfortable in your own skin.

Carry-over like this can be difficult to live with because your 'real' life seems like a dream, as if something is always missing. You're constantly searching, certain that there is some great meaning to your life, but unable to discover what it might be.

Suddenly, you meet someone, and although there's no physical chemistry between you, there is, nevertheless, a strong connection. You feel this person could hold some answers, and maybe you feel like you owe them something, and that they hold the key to your purpose in life. You start to 'imagine' scenarios where you've met them before, or they tell you something from their past that resonates within your soul. What's going on? You never met this person, and yet you know them. They aren't like you, you don't seem like a good match, yet you know you'll be friends for life.

Are you going mad? No, you're not. This is someone you made a contract to help before this lifetime. You and your past life angels discussed a way that you could fulfill your promises (see my book *Past Life Angels* published by O Books). All you have to do is remember. Once you do, life will change, because you'll know, and hopefully when you remember what it is, you'll do what you promised you'd do before you came here. The 'something' that was missing will come winging into place like a lost piece of a jigsaw puzzle, and everything will fit.

You'll stop wasting your life looking for what you're meant to be doing, and experience a freedom that few people manage to enjoy.

Such a relationship developed in my life. I met a man called Graham, who had been searching for a meaning to his life. I had started writing song lyrics after I'd had my own past life awakening. (Described in my book *Souls Don't Lie* published by O Books). I couldn't write music, so I needed a composer to add the melodies to my words. I had a fair amount of success, which in itself was amazing, as I was such a fledgling. One song, *I'm Still Falling* (written with Barry Upton) actually earned a silver disc.

Graham seemed like a gift from God (as indeed he proved to be, although maybe not quite as I'd imagined him to be), as he lived near to me, and was as prodigious with his composing as I was with my lyrics.

It was a bit puzzling in a way as he was most certainly not a fan of the country music genre and my lyrics tended to lean that way, but anyway we managed to co-write several lovely songs. After a while I explained why I leaned towards country, having recently discovered my past life connection to the country music giant, Garth Brooks. I told Graham a little about my story, and my dream of having it published as a book, and my disappointment at having (at that stage) no luck in finding a commercial publisher who was willing to take it on. Graham asked to read the manuscript. At that point, Tony (my husband) and I made our sudden, past life prompted decision to move from Norfolk to Somerset, and in the move we accidentally lost touch with Graham.

Six months later, to our amazement, he tracked us down, and we never really did find out how, because he'd had no idea where we were, except that we were somewhere in Somerset. It seemed that something very powerful was driving him.

Having read the manuscript of my story, at the time called

Ripples, Graham announced that he wanted to sponsor the publication of the book out of his own pocket. I was delighted of course, but also mystified. Why? I asked him and he answered, cryptically, "For love."

He also said that he 'knew' the story. He said it moved him, and he felt he had to help me with it. He said it was a story that needed to be told.

It was a puzzle, but a pleasing one. It rather restored my faith in human nature. We went ahead and the book, in its original format, was published in the UK. We both knew that we had to speak to Garth Brooks before could be released in the USA, because the last thing we wanted was to offend him. The three of us, me, Tony (my husband) and Graham made a plan to go together to the USA. But, before we went, we knew we needed to get some answers. It looked as if the only way to discover the answers was through regression. By taking Graham back to that time, the time of *Ripples,* we hoped to find out what the real connection between us was.

*

Spiritual love

Graham: *It's sometime in the 1600s. I'm in a hurry, but something important has to take place before I can leave. I'm aged about 27, and male. I've got long blond hair and my name is Jared. Next to me stands Ryan, Irish, tall and dark and burly, he's my best friend. We're standing at the back of a church, near Middleton, it's an abbey really. We're dressed in white shirts, breeches and boots. Up near the altar there's a farmer and his wife and daughter, and a clergyman, who's fidgeting. I think he's in more of a hurry than I am...*

The altar looks beautiful. It should do, we were up half the night gathering flowers and candles. You'd never know the abbey wasn't in use. We're waiting for her, Madeleine. The door opens and she comes inside. She's very pretty, fair hair, blue eyes, slim and young. She's dressed in blue – flowers in her hair. She doesn't even seem to see me. She only has eyes for Ryan, and he for her. I wasn't sure about this marriage, this secret and possibly dangerous arrangement, but seeing how they look at each other, I think it just has to be, whatever the consequences. But, I am afraid for my friend.

Later

The marriage vows have been made, the clergyman has fled. Madeleine turns to me with her eyes bright and teary. She smiles. My personal preference lies in the other, male gender, but, I can accept what Ryan sees in her. Her energy is light and bright, and God knows he needs that. I start to say that I must leave. My sister and my whole family need me. Ryan grasps my arm and gestures me apart from the happy group. He is my dearest friend, my sometimes defender, and I'd do anything for him. He says, quietly, "Promise me. If anything happens…take care of her for me." He nods towards his new wife. "Of course," I answer. It's one of those off-the-cuff promises a person makes, meaning it, but not realizing it would soon be called in.

Madeleine's step-mother, Margaret, hates my friend, Ryan, with such intensity that I'm not surprised that he is a little paranoid about his future safety. There are almost no lengths she would go to, to get rid of him, and now he's eloped with Madeleine, marrying her against their wishes, I suppose anything could happen. (I was to realize later that I actually had no idea just how ruthless and evil she could be.)

We shake hands, and with my thoughts turning to home, I walk away with a wave, and untie my horse. I get on, and with a kick of my heels we're off at a gallop, on the long journey home to Wales.

Next important event.

It's two years later, and I'm back, back in Hambledon, where my friend Ryan had made his home with his new wife, and I don't know how things could have gone so badly, so quickly. I knew they would face trouble, but I am very distressed to find that Ryan's fate has been sealed so finally by that hateful bitch, Margaret. She killed him with her orders as surely as if she'd wielded the sword herself. He died on some battlefield, fighting someone else's war. But poor Madeleine, I never expected to find her dead too. She killed herself at his loss, poor child. I should have been here. I promised him to take care of her. I feel awful at having let my friend down.

*

Graham: Now I understand, the 'love' I talked about, was love for my friend, Ryan, and the feeling that I had was to make up for letting his trust in me down. Jenny, as Madeleine, and I, as Jared, shared a love for her lover, and my friend, that has come through to this life. We'll always have an unbroken bond because of this.

Now, I'm very glad I was able to make good my promise, even if it had to wait over 300 years. I feel more settled now. I still wanted to meet 'Ryan' again, but I knew it would be difficult to accomplish. Big stars like Garth Brooks are put behind barriers and the real world can rarely intrude. I can see that they need protecting, but sometimes it makes them miss important things too, because the people trying to reach them with news are kept behind that barrier.

Since I discovered my past and have been able to do what I came here to do, life has changed, or more accurately I have changed my life for the better. I finally ended a barren and soulless marriage, started a blues band, which was very successful, found a new partner and moved to Spain. Quite a lot of changes have taken place, and all due to that one realization.

*

This regression explained it all. Graham felt he had failed to live up to his promises to Ryan to care for Madeleine in that lifetime as Jared, and so he was determined to do it in this life, and help her, as me, Jenny. It also explains why, despite being unlikely friends in some ways, this does reflect the past too, and explains why we are in fact very close friends. It also explained some of the events that happened when we went on our trip to the USA and met Garth.

When we arrived in Nashville we had an hour long meeting with Garth's manager, Bob Doyle, and his attorney, Rusty Jones. One question they asked was, "So, if Garth says this is all true, will you consider him to be your husband?" Although that made us laugh, it just about indicated where they were coming from, and why they wouldn't help us. After a difficult conversation, we succeeded in our need to convince them that I was genuine. They finally conceded that I was sincere in my beliefs, and we shook hands, but answered very firmly in the negative when I asked if they would help me meet him, so that he could judge the story for himself.

So, the most important person we needed approval from was Garth himself. Through a series of synchronistic events we did indeed manage to talk to him one to one. (*Ripples* has now been re-written and republished as *Souls Don't Lie* – published by O Books). The regression explained a lot of what was said at that meeting, and particularly it explained why Garth seemed to feel no embarrassment or reticence at strongly implying that Graham was gay. (He isn't). It's not something you could normally do with a stranger, but of course what Garth was feeling was his past life connection as Ryan to Jared (Graham's past life persona), who *was* a homosexual.

All this has had even more far-reaching effects, because one of the things I had contracted to do before I came to this life was to reawaken Garth, so that his 'training' as Ryan, wouldn't be forgotten. His life has also changed dramatically since we met. He too left a marriage that had drifted, found a new partner and retired from the business so that he can be the best father to his children.

I personally realized my life-long dream of making my own independent living as a writer, which came just in time to support Tony through some medical problems and surgery. I also found passion and fulfillment in my remembered role as a spiritual seed-planter.

*

I'm Living Two Lives

Caroline found it difficult to sleep and do her job properly, because so many flashes of past images kept coming to her mind. Certain that there was a past life reason for this, I sent her to see Barry Laine.

Caroline: *I found myself in some sort of concentration camp. People all around me, dressed in medieval clothes, were terrified, and dying. I was the boss's woman and I was wearing sackcloth. I was not allowed to see what was happening outside, but I could hear it. I had two children, one older and one a baby, by the boss. Before I came here I had a husband and family. But the soldiers came and killed my father. My husband had been forced to run away, and so I only had my mother and my sister, Ria. I died in that camp.*

Next

I went back into the life before the camp, looking into my body as a baby in that same lifetime, somewhere in northern Europe. I was aware that I was very cold and hungry, and I could see a pine tree towering over me. From time to time my mother or my sister Ria, would come and check up on me.

Previous Life

I went even further back into another previous life when I was an Indian Warrior called 'Run-Like-The-Wind'. I was looking for my braves. I was the runner and a protector of my people. I was not the chief of the tribe, but once I had proved my bravery and married my bride-to-be, the old chief would step down, and I would take his place. My bride was beautiful and I had no doubt that my hunting trip would prove me to be braver than all the others.

Suddenly everything went wrong, and I realized we had become surrounded by our enemies from another tribe. I started shaking as I saw them killing my braves.

(Barry said I was actually crying at this point.) I said, "I must go now into the desert to save my people," and my legs started to shake and then there was silence. I died in the desert trying to save my people, and I knew I had failed.

Barry: Two more sessions were arranged to bury the past lives, and bring Caroline's treatment to a close.

Caroline: I'm no longer troubled by past images and I feel like a new CD has been placed in my mind, and the old one destroyed.

Caroline had obviously brought through a lot of guilt about what she saw as her responsibilities in her past lives. She had really been helpless and the victim of circumstances, but in her own mind she had been a failure. All the spontaneous flashes she was experiencing were her soul's way, her past life angel's way, of trying to wake her up. This was because she really needed to forgive herself and understand that she had done her best, always, given her limitations. Now she'll stop going down dead-ends in her life and re-write her own script, which can do nothing but enhance her current life. She may well encounter some of the people she experienced her past lives with too, and be able to help them in this life, which will improve her own happiness.

CHAPTER 11

Family Circles

You're very close to your family, but sometimes you really wish you weren't. Life seems very complicated and you always seem to be getting involved in the problems of other members of your family. You feel drawn to them and yet repelled sometimes, tied by something older than your life which keeps you unable to progress your own life as you'd like to. You feel vaguely disapproved of, you're always trying to make the other members of your family happy, but it's never enough.

Families really do often go round in circles, life after life, always thinking that this time things would be put right, and yet, because everyone in the family has a different agenda, things always go pear-shaped. It would be great to do group family regressions, and then all the knots could be untangled, the 'Is' dotted and the 'Ts' crossed, but usually you have to resort to sorting out one person at a time.

Animal Instinct

June had suffered from an eating disorder in her mid-thirties and mild obsessive compulsive disorder. She was anxious to prevent a recurrence by finding the cause of her problems and healing them. Her mother had been obese and did a lot of comfort eating, and several members of her family seemed to have similar habits, so this seemed to be a case of 'family circles', where they were all involved in the same past life together. I sent June to see the regression therapist Judith Hubbard.

June: *When Judith took me down the pathway looking for the relevant past life door, I experienced a lot of subconscious resistance, and floated upwards, away from the doors. However, she overcame this and I eventually found the door.*

It was old, with rotting wood. I went through, but when Judith asked me to close it behind me, it was difficult to shut as it was warped. Once I was through, Judith directed me to look at my feet and for a moment I couldn't speak. I was too shocked. I saw not feet at all, but huge paws! Then I realized that I was a young lion. I had never expected to be an animal!

Later

Judith took me forward to a significant point in that lifetime ... and I was an old male lion, the leader. Around me were a group of lions and they were angry with me. We were in a dry, barren place, and I had led them to this place with no food. I'd done it with the best intentions, moving the pride away from human hunters, but I'd taken the wrong pathway. One lion that I recognized as my mother in my present life, came up very close and she was furious. I could communicate telepathically with the pride and I felt horrible and distressing emotion. I felt their anger, and I was very sad because as their leader, I'd failed them badly. They were going to die because of me.

I became very emotional as I increasingly felt their anger and fear. It became very difficult for Judith to communicate with me. In the far distance I could see a man with a spear. The other lions pounced on me and bit my neck, and I felt terrible pain. I cried out, not fighting back, because I felt they were justified in killing me, but at the same time sad that I was letting them to do it.

I saw a bright light, and knew that I had died. I followed Judith's instructions and looked back at my lion body, reviewing that life, looking for the lessons it contained. I was surrounded by a wide beam of golden, white light. There was a loving figure, which I felt was Jesus or somebody equally enlightened. He enveloped me in a comforting and healing energy.

*

Judith: June having this experience of being an animal was a surprise to me, but it was important not to allow this information to disrupt the session, so I carried on as normal. At the end, I brought her back through that lifetime and back through the door. This time it shut easily behind her and it was no longer warped. Despite the shock of such an unexpected experience it has given her a lot of insight into her anorexia and she says she found the experience very positive. She no longer comfort eats and she is much more assertive and confident.

June: Since my 'lion' experience I don't use food as an issue when something goes wrong anymore, and I also realize that it is OK to be more assertive now, and that I shouldn't give my power away. I have blossomed immensely, spiritually. I also know now, since talking to Jenny on the phone, that I have a powerful, 'golden lion inside me' and that I shouldn't be afraid to let it out sometimes!

*

Some people don't believe that we can come here as animals, but it makes a lot of sense. There are some scenarios that will only work if you're an animal, and it's logical that experience enables you to gradually rise up the food chain, until you're ready to handle the human condition. This doesn't imply which species has the most evolved soul, just that the human condition seems to be the most difficult in which to maintain a spiritual connection, so it makes sense that it would be the last one we had to cope with. However, I've also seen evidence that people can go back to being animals after having been a human, which only goes to show that the universe is more complicated than we as humans can entirely understand.

*

Trapped Going Round and Round

Elizabeth didn't really like most of the family she'd been left with at age 45. Her Dad had been a bit emotionally weak, but a lovely man. Mum had been a bit critical, but her love was sorely missed. Once both parents had passed on, her sister was the closest one left, and the two of them had never gotten along. Elizabeth and her sister gradually became estranged. The sister wasn't spiritually minded, so it never seemed to worry her, but Elizabeth was a developing spiritual soul and wanted to see if she could find answers for their problems from their past lives together.

It had all started centuries ago, and if Elizabeth hadn't discovered the story, and jumped off the merry-go-round, it would have gone on and on and on. Ever since they were small, Elizabeth's sister had seemingly resented her, and Elizabeth, a happy-go-lucky child, had never known why.

Elizabeth: *I'm in a cold place, cold but sunny. There's snow higher on the hills. In front of the village on the other side is a fjord. I have long blond hair in pigtails and I'm wearing a sort of pinafore dress with a furry coat and boots.*

(At this point Elizabeth recognized an older woman as being her current life sister).

The whole village is in turmoil, people trying to fit more belongings onto the already full carts, fires burning homes, and clothes and children sitting at the track-side, crying and bewildered. We're all sacrificing our belongings so that we can escape.

Later

She's as stubborn as always. There are only a very few of us adults left who haven't gone down with the sickness. We have to abandon the village, or we'll all die. It should be burnt to the ground, not a thing left above ground, but she refuses to leave. She sits in her shack and won't come out. I argue with her for hours, but she won't come. She's my mother. I could stay with her, but what's the point? I'd rather go with the others than die here alone with her. I am torn and don't know what to do, but then I decide, I don't want to die, so I'm going! The others want to burn her hut too, but she won't come out and I won't let them fire it with her inside. We're all arguing and struggling, but finally they agree to leave her alive. Is that the best thing? I don't know. I don't know.

Later

As we leave I look back and see her face at the window. She screamed and cried when I said I was leaving, but still she wouldn't budge. She must have heard me fighting for her life, but still she wouldn't come out. I've made sure she has enough food to see out the winter, but I doubt she'll survive. If the cold or the sickness doesn't get her, likely the animals will. But I refuse to think about it. I owe the rest of the village too. I get on the last wagon and we roll away. I doubt I'll ever see her again.

Next Life

I'm so happy. I'm to be married. My name is Jenny, it's London in 1824, and I'm to become Mrs Gregory Linderman tomorrow. I've always wanted to be married, and at last my day has come. Gregory is very handsome and important. I will have a good life as his wife. We'll have many children, sons, and I'll make him very happy. Life is wonderful.

Later (12 months after the wedding took place)

Now I'm terrified. I'm pregnant and no one will tell me what's to happen to me. I don't know how the baby will come out. I can feel it growing in my stomach, but I feel threatened by it. How will it come out? I don't see how. Will they have to cut me? I'm so scared and no one will tell me. The only good thing is that Gregory treats me as if I am very precious. I hope it's a son though, he wants a son.

Later

I'm in agony. I'm giving birth. I never dreamed it would be like this or

I would never have allowed Gregory near me. The baby is forcing its way out of my body. It's impossible! It's trying to kill me. The pain is unbelievable. I doubt I will survive.

Something very strange is happening to me. I'm leaving the world. Everything is turning dark. I'm not scared now. I can hear a part of me talking to my baby, telling her that this time she will live and I will die. I'll die so that she can live. This will make up for some tragic time long past when I left her, my mother, to die alone. I hope Gregory treats his daughter well, even though she's not the son he longs for. I feel the baby resents me for her being a girl, but I couldn't change that...could I?

Next Life

Why is she so cruel? She married my father just out of spite and to become an important person. She never loved him, she only loved his money and his name, and she's making him so unhappy. She hates me because my father loves me. I try hard to please her for father's sake, but nothing ever really pleases her.

Later

She hates my new husband and makes any excuse to be hateful to him. If he didn't love me, he'd leave. I feel guilty that he stays and suffers her abuse, just to be with me, but I don't feel I can leave and he won't ever leave without me.

Later

She's had my husband, my lover, my soul mate, stolen away and sent him to be killed. My life is over, because of her. I'm going to leave this world. I can't be here without him. I'm climbing to a cliff-top and standing here on the brink, a strange thought comes to mind. I know I died once so that she might live, and yet still she hates me. I gave her life and sacrificed my own. I thought she'd be grateful, but she hates me so much, for one time when I left her to die. I'm falling, falling, down and down, through the air and into my husband's arms.

*

From her regressions Elizabeth could clearly see that trying to make amends and appease the unhappy soul of her sister in this life was useless, and she would be better off to cut the cord that bound them together. Coming back time after time to try and put things right wasn't working. She had done all she could and it was time for her to move on, even if her sister couldn't. This regression proved that guilt is the most useless of all emotions. Elizabeth couldn't have a good relationship with her sister, but at least now she was free to make her own life, without any regrets.

Now, if Elizabeth meets this same soul again, in her next lifetime, she won't make the same mistakes and will stay away from her right from the start. Because her intention, while in between lives, will be to stop trying over and over, and to achieve separation. Her past life angel will make sure they don't come back together again as blood relatives. We really can't walk anyone else's path for them, and in the end our main responsibility has to be to our own spirit.

*

Elizabeth: Now I can see that my sister's hatred for me came from long, long ago. Despite my trying to make up to her for what I did many lives and many centuries ago, she can't forgive. She never forgave me for leaving her when she was my mother, even though she was stubborn and I wanted her to leave. Even though I stopped the other villagers from killing her, she never forgave me for abandoning her. Then, even though I gave her life, and died that she might live, she resented me for her being a girl. I expect she didn't have a very good life as Gregory's only child, a disappointment. At least now I can understand and I know what to do. If I can't make peace with this soul, if she won't soften towards me, then I'll have to stay away from her, as her negativity from her is harming my spirit.

CHAPTER 12

Ill Health

Sometimes past lives can cause actual physical manifestations, such as the recreation of scars, illness, disability and disease. You might also have a birthmark indicating the site of a previous injury.

In my book, *Past Life Angels*, I describe how we get nudges to wake us up to our past lives. These nudges can sometimes take the form of illness or physical problems and if this is the case, they can involve a certain amount of synchronicity as an extra clue. For instance if you died aged 50 from a dagger to the throat, then at age 50 in the next life it's possible that this trauma will be recreated by your body.

One man I know of who had died in the 1640s aged nineteen, from a sword wound to the stomach, had a car accident aged nineteen in this lifetime, and as he put it, "a piece of the car body broke off, and I was skewered."

This was the modern day recreation of the original injury.

Knowing this kind of information can give you tremendous opportunities for healing the past. In the case of this man, he hadn't woken up to his spiritual purpose in this lifetime, and the recurrence and re-creation of his scars from the previous life was a very forceful reminder of that.

If you have an illness, chronic or acute, or some troubling symptoms that doctors don't seem to be able to help you with, consider looking deeper into yourself to find the possible causes. It's quite possible that it could be an acute wake up call and that if you don't take the right action you may develop a more serious illness.

*

One woman wrote and told me that she was very depressed at Christmas time because every single year, for all her life, she had become ill in time for Christmas. It was ruining her enjoyment of the festive season and her family had come to call it, 'the Christmas Curse'.

It turned out that she had been a young soldier in WWII. The soldier had been due to go 'over the top' (into close combat battle), and would be facing almost certain death, on 26th December. In order for the soldier to subconsciously try and avoid his fate, he had developed a psychosomatic illness on 25th December – Christmas Day. The illness seemed very real to him, but had actually been created in his mind. In any case it was not enough to save him, so he had been sent out to fight, and was cut down by enemy fire at the age of eighteen.

Naturally this trauma had come through into this life, but instead of the war being blamed, Christmas itself became the trigger, so the psychosomatic illness had been recreated every year as the anniversary of his violent death approached, in a vain effort to avoid it.

It's possible for you to carry through into your current lifetime, the connection of the soul that will allow a past-life condition to re-manifest itself in your current life. This will be a condition that was rooted in some conflict that you left unresolved in a previous life. This condition and its physical manifestation will probably have been repeated over many lifetimes, because still the under-lying cause, the unfinished business, hasn't been finished.

*

Inexplicable Pain

Kylie had experienced terrible stomach pains in the left side of her abdomen, from the age of fourteen. She had visited the doctor several times but no cause was found. After pregnancy and child-birth the pains got very severe again, and this time they were blamed on the fact that she given birth by Caesarean section. She was told she would just have to live with the pain. A few years later the pain was so debilitating that she had to spend many days of the week, crouched on the sofa with a hot water bottle clutched to her stomach. Her life was a mess. She couldn't make any arrangements or commitments for fear of having to let people down, because there was never any knowing when the pain was going to come.

Finally, as a last resort she tried regression therapy. She was regressed by Katrina Pleasance (who is no longer working as a regression therapist).

Kylie: *I'm in the countryside around Sunderland. I'm making my way on a horse through some trees, and ahead of me the land opens out. A rising hill of thick long green grass appears. Running around on it are several groups of men. They're struggling together, and some of them have swords. I ride into the middle of the battle, looking, searching desperately for a certain face. My brother is somewhere here in this one-sided battle, and if I don't hurry it will be too late. I don't care about my safety. I've promised our mother that I'll take care of Andrew, her baby son. As the firstborn he's my responsibility. But I can't find him. My mother always trusted me to look out for him. I have betrayed her trust. I should have known he'd go. I should have stopped him. I should never have been so stupid.*

Moments Later

I still can't find him. There are bloody bodies, unrecognizable, all over the grass. There are pairs of men grappling with each other. The hillside echoes with their grunts, cries of pain and the gasps of their dying breaths. I turn my horse round and round, dodging the skirmishes, but still I can't find him.

Moments Later

Some of the men have noticed me in their midst and they're attacking me now. How am I to find Andrew now? I'm going to fail. Too late, I start to fight back. It's too late now. I'm overwhelmed by numbers. A sword goes through me. It feels cold at first and then a terrible burning feeling rises from the wound. Suddenly I'm on the grass. I don't recall falling or hitting the ground. Now the blood on the grass is mine and it's just white agony. The light is fading. I've failed my mother. Now she'll have to bury two sons, if she ever finds out what happened to us…

*

It transpired that Kylie had spent most of this lifetime thinking about looking for her younger brother. He'd been given up for adoption when she was only three years old. Kylie had never forgiven herself, even though of course there was nothing she could have done to stop what happened at that young age. She hadn't been able to get any information from her parents because they had both died when she was ten, and then she had been fostered. Andrew, the brother from the past, was her brother again in this life, and she felt like she'd lost him again, she'd failed to protect him again. Now she had been given another chance to find him and resolve her guilt, and with it came the unexplained pain, which was merely a nudge to remind her of who she'd been, and the powerful loyalty she felt towards her brother.

*

Kylie: I'd never had any luck tracking down my baby brother.

I'd tried asking around where we were born, in Kent, but had no answers. I didn't have enough information for the authorities to help, and I'd pretty much given up by the time I was about 20. My memories of him and what little my parents had told me, were from when I was only aged three to ten, so it was difficult. Now, aged 30, I wanted to give it another try. I understood why now. It seemed obvious that my brother Sam, was the same one, Andrew, who I'd failed to find in that previous life. This time I wouldn't fail him.

Kylie: This was where the regression worked some real magic. I understood that my past life angel had been nudging me with the pain, so that I'd recall my death and where it had happened, because that place was important. Sunderland! I was being drawn back to that place for a reason, I was sure that I'd find him in Sunderland, right where I'd lost him, and I was right. I put ads in all the local papers and it all came together with incredible speed. Within two weeks I'd heard from him, and just another week on, I finally met my brother, Sam.

That's when another miracle happened. From the day I put my arms around my brother, my abdominal pain vanished. It's never come back.

*

War Wounds

Joan had a pain in her left shoulder and the left side of her upper back, for which no medical reason could be found. She asked to be able to try regression therapy as a last resort, and I sent her to see Kathy Gibbons.

Joan: *Kathy first asked me to put all my conscious awareness into my shoulder and back. Then she told me to stay with the pain and tell her what thoughts went with it. I was wounded and abandoned.*

The Early Part of that Life

I'm six years old and I live in Scotland. I'm playing with my little brother and two sisters and my sister's and neighbors' kids. My family is poor but Ma and Pa are loving parents. We live in a small cottage, but we're very happy.

Later

It's 1915 and I'm queuing up with some friends to join the army, and Ma and Pa are there to see me off. I go to a camp where I'm in uniform training. We're being prepared for war, and suddenly it doesn't seem like such a good idea. I can't get out of it now though.

Later

We are at Gallipoli, fighting our way up the beaches. I'm lying on my stomach and there's smoke and bodies everywhere. All I can hear are terrible shrieks and the moans of the injured. Hell has come to earth.

I'm walking over dead bodies, and then suddenly I'm with a group of strangers, staggering away from the war zone. We walk up into the mountains, when I suddenly become aware of the agony I'm in. I have a hole in the left side of my back where I was hit by a shell in battle but have only become aware of the pain now. I'm with other walking wounded and we stumble on. I'm desperately frightened.

Later

We've been found. Some of the men are very badly injured and they're being attended to, but no one sees me. I'm very weak and I watch while the trucks take the wounded away. I cry for help but no one hears me and I watch them drive away. I'm not going to make it as my blood is soaking my clothes and I'm slipping away. I think of my family and am overcome by deep sadness as they'll never know where I died.

Moving On

I find myself in a place in the spirit realms where I see my family and say what I wanted to say all those years ago. I tell them how much I love them and we all hug. I feel at peace.

Healing

Kathy brings me out of the regression for healing on my left side and I take up the position I was in when hit by the shell – I'm kneeling taking aim as if holding a rifle. Kathy pushes a small metal candle holder against the left side of my back under my shoulder and says. "Feel this pressure from the shell and I want you to press against me until the pain's gone."

I do so for several minutes and then I remove the metal from my back to make sure the wound is healed. Kathy tells me to do a mental scan of my body and to tell her if I have any heavy energy or blocks. I don't and my body feels wonderfully clear now.

Kathy: I explained to Joan that even emotional past life trauma could bring through physical signs and symptoms to her current life. The pains are there as reminders to take steps to release old traumas. Now that Joan has healed the origin of her pain in her past life, she'll be able to let it go.

Joan: After the session, the very next day, I felt centered, clear, and light-hearted, without any blocked feelings. Another month later, and the pain in my back was completely gone.

This pain that Joan had brought through is a classic symptom of a past life that needs revealing and healing. It was the hardship, the devastation and the misery that had lived on in Joan's soul after her body in that life had succumbed.

In this life the shoulder pain was a nudge from her past life angel to wake up and take notice. Past life memories can be stored all over the body, for while the mind is confined to the brain, the soul can roam where it chooses.

CHAPTER 13

Bad Luck and Guilt

You feel cursed, because it seems everything in life goes wrong for you. You've never won anything – the lottery, a raffle or even at bingo. You feel that just as you're about to succeed or take a step up, something always comes along and knocks you back down. You start to accept that the only kind of luck you have is bad luck, and you get into a state of mind where all you expect is for things to go wrong, and things do go wrong – continuously.

This is often a self-fulfilling prophesy, caused by that most destructive of emotional blocks – guilt. The more negative you feel the more you attract negative outcomes, because universal energy is magnetic. Having guilt about actions you took in a previous life is very common, but quite unnecessary. To feel guilt at things you did when we were at a lower level of soul evolution is as nonsensical as a bird feeling guilty about something it did when it was a dinosaur.

I Shouldn't Have Been Glad

Ruby wanted to be regressed because she had felt inexplicable guilt all her life and wanted to see if past life regression would solve it.

I sent her to see Barbara Ford-Hammond.

Ruby: *There's a clearing of tropical trees, and a waterfall. It's the 1950s and I'm wearing a bikini. I'm jumping in the water. It's like a deep canyon. I'm about 25 years old. I'm alone at the minute. I think I'm on holiday. It might be a sort of jungle but this is a very private and exclusive area. I'm drying myself down. It's really warm. I'm walking though to some huts. Holiday huts. I'm definitely on holiday. There's a cocktail waiting for me. I must have a lot of money. There's a man in my bedroom. He's lying in a towel on the bed, reading a bloke's magazine. He's good looking. We're both quite glamorous and wealthy. He's wearing a lot of gold. He's rich. Probably there's a lot of stuff about him that I don't need to know. He doesn't tell me a lot about it. I think he's up to no good.*

Later

I'm brushing my hair. It's brown and I'm tanned. He's got champagne. Mine's a martini made with fruit. I like it here. We're here for a month. We get away a lot.

Later

We go back to London. I'm a bit bored here. I don't have any real job to do, and really I don't think I like him that much. He doesn't like me to do stuff, just look glamorous on his arm. He's older than me. I lunch a lot in places like the Savoy, and posh hotels in London. All I have to occupy myself is the fashion of the day and what to spend his money on. It might sound like a good life, but it's boring sometimes.

Next

I'm in Piccadilly Circus on my own. It's all very busy. I'm in the middle, with everything spinning around me like a whirlwind. I feel confused. I need to slow it down. I'm sitting down now with my head in my hands, trying to stop things from going so fast. People are looking at me funny. I'm panicking, not sure where I'm going. I'm about 25-30 and out on my own. There's something wrong. I know there's something wrong.

Next

I'm buying a newspaper. There's been a plane crash. I'm thinking that maybe my husband might have been on the plane, but I'm not that bothered. Is that awful?

I don't think he was a very good person. I don't really know what he got up to. He did a lot of traveling. Well, I'll do what I like now. I don't have to go to any more lunches with all those silly cows who were the wives of his friends. I feel really happy to be free. But I also feel guilty because I feel really happy.

Later

He was on the plane. All I can think is that I'm going to be very rich now, as he'll have left his money to me. I'm a bit worried as well. Who knows where some of it was, and how he earned it? Will there be any repercussions? Is someone going to claim the money is theirs or owed to them? I just don't know. I think I'll just grab the money and go away for a year or maybe even more – I've no children, and no boss, so I can do what I like now.

Later

My hair is tied back, long and grey. The room's dark. I'm writing goodbye letters to friends. I've got an illness but I don't know what. I'm only young still, in my fifties. I've got a nurse, she's younger than me. There's probably not much for me to do here now. I'll end my letters now and then lie down and go to sleep. Not even sure if I'll wake up tomorrow. I'm not in pain.

Later

I've not got long. I think I've got cancer. (Whispers) Probably because I was glad when my husband died. I don't really feel frightened. The nurse has come in to pull the curtains like any other day. She doesn't stay over. She's going now. I'll just have a drink of water. I feel like I should have a last drink of vodka or something. I wonder if the nurse has got some. I'll look in the cupboard. There's some whisky there, a nice one. I think I'll have some and savor it – mmm. Feel a bit woozy now I've not had a drink for ages. It's quite pleasant. I think I'll just go to sleep.

Barbara: Ruby's regression touches on the guilt that she thought she should have felt and that certainly seems to be an issue with her sometimes, as it is with many women in one way or another. She said the experience has given her much to think about and she will be clearer in her thoughts now. She definitely won't be tied or trapped with anyone she doesn't care about.

Ruby: I learned a lot. It's important for me to be a free person. I felt guilty because my husband had died, but he wasn't a very good person and he didn't really treat me very well, and then I was glad to be free of him. I need to trust myself. Trust my own instincts. I don't need to be lost. I just need to spend sometime thinking about it.

*

I Feel Like I Was Evil

Bridget felt very isolated and lonely in this world. She felt she had to spend her whole life making everything right for everyone else, ignoring her own needs. She felt the time had come to get some answers, so I sent her to see Fiona Shields.

Bridget: *It's the year 238 BCE, and I'm on the island of Corsica. I'm a very big, strong and tall, masculine man – a Roman soldier, wearing sandals with straps across my feet and up the ankles. I'm also wearing heavy amour. I'm outdoors, and there's fighting. I can hear the clang of heavy swords, and I can smell blood. I have a heavy shield in one hand and a sword in the other.*

Oh my God! I'm fighting and killing people. There's death everywhere and I'm full of fear. As I look around at the carnage, I feel physically sick. It's horrible, horrible.

I hate what I'm doing and what I've done. I shake my head. I have to get out of here. This killing isn't right. I want to get away from it. I hate it and I hate myself, but I can't seem to get away from it. When I think of all those that died at my hand, my head hurts, my stomach feels sick, and I'm beginning to shake all over. I'm really sorry for what I've done.

I've taken so many lives. How can I ever feel good inside again? I was following orders, but that doesn't make it any more right to kill and maim like I've just done.

(I got very emotional at this point and cried deeply for a couple of minutes.)

I'm getting up now and walking away. I'm just walking away on my own. People call out to me to stop and come back, but I ignore them. My head is bowed because I'm so ashamed, and I just keep walking away. I can't look back. I don't want to look back at the death and devastation I've caused. I'm having difficulty moving because I feel heavy with pain. I don't want to see anybody. I don't know where I'm going. It's misty, there's no light, and nothing to show me where to go. I'm by a river now. I sit down and hang my head in shame. I can see the water flowing at my feet and I just want to flow away with it. I feel defeated.

Later
I don't know what to do now. There's no one around to ask. I wish I knew where to go. I wish I had somebody to turn to. I wish I had someone who cared for me. Who would want me now after all I've done? I don't want to go on, I'd rather die. I'm getting weak and I feel so helpless. I'm lying down. My head's spinning. I feel so alone and so afraid.

Later
I hear the thump of horse's hooves coming towards me and suddenly I'm surrounded by soldiers. They've come to get me because I deserted the camp. They're laughing at me and trying to decide what to do with me. I don't feel so fearful any more. I don't care if they kill me. I'd rather die than go through another battle.

Later
They put a rope over a branch of a tree near by. They pull the heavy armor from my body and put me up on a horse and place the noose

around my neck. I'm not afraid though my stomach feels a bit sick. Now my neck's sore because the noose is getting tighter. It'll be over soon. They kick the horse and I dangle, choking. Then I'm gone from that body and I feel peaceful. It's all over now.

Fiona asks me what lessons I learned from that lifetime. I reply, "Never hurt another human being. All life is precious, even down to the life of a fly. You have to forgive, forgive everything. I don't have to be so fearful and I don't have to be afraid. I have the strength. I no longer have to be paralyzed with fear.

*

Fiona says: Watching Bridget going through her experience was a privilege in a strange way. I felt I was there with her watching the devastation, it felt extremely real. I could see that this past life experience was extremely deep as her whole body wracked with the pain and tears of it. She looked ten years younger after the session and left smiling and feeling lighter and brighter in herself.

Bridget says: At the end of the session I felt so much lighter in myself. I felt a big shift in my energy and realize that everyone is on their own path, their own journey and I can't do everything for everyone.

*

I Failed Them

Dean wanted to know more about what made him the person he is today, and why he felt that there was something important he should be doing with his life, so I sent him to see Diane Egby.

Dean: I was on my way to a very significant event, something earth-changing. I was walking along a hillside, looking down on trees and a blue lake. I was in the Middle East, and yet it was so lush and green that it must have been long, long ago. I was male with short brown hair and a beard, dressed in red and white robes and sandals. I was walking with the aid of a cane, weary.

Later

I'd walked for days. I was on some kind of pilgrimage because I carried no supplies and I had been fed along the way by villagers. I just knew instinctively that there was some event I had to get to, and I had a feeling of great urgency. I could see hills in the distance and knew I was only about a day away from my goal. I felt very joyful at the prospect. It was the start of a new age, and I was excited about what I would witness.

Later

I found myself in a busy, dusty street. I went inside a temple and there in a polished marble-lined room, I reached my quest. It was The Ark of the Covenant! That's what I had come to see. The power was amazing, filling my body with energy. I tried to grasp what it was. Not the energy of God, as people thought. It was the energy of love – pure love. It was gold, with tapering sides, wider at the top than the bottom. There were handles on each corner so that it could be carried by four men. The power ran through me, making me very emotional, to the point of tears.

Later

I was sitting on a rock under a very hot sun, surrounded by red sand. I was very thirsty and old and tired. I felt sad because I was going back to my village and they were hoping that I was going to bring them good news about the savior coming, but I didn't have that news. In my mind's eye I could see that as I approached the village, people would come towards me, happy, expecting the news that the savior was coming, but instead I will have to tell them that he has been crucified.

Later

Lying down with people around crying. I wasn't sad. I was so tired. I gently slipped away and I looked back to see them carrying my body away to be burnt. I didn't care what they did with it – it wasn't me. Suddenly I was going up, very fast, exploding upwards...

*

Diane: Guilt is a useless emotion, and its only purpose is in the moment, to tell us that we've done something wrong. If held onto as in Dean's case, it can become like a drug and hook us to it. Dean needs to concentrate on the amazing experience of seeing the Ark. This will allow him to open to the other experiences it would have triggered in that life, and give up the guilt. I could feel the whole room electrify during his recall and I have no doubt it was real and profound.

Dean: The memories that came up gave me an absolute belief that there is reincarnation. I feel I failed my people, because I didn't bring them the news they wanted, but I was respected. I still have some underlying sadness and I'll be undergoing some more sessions to try and root it out completely.

*

It's not very pleasant to discover that in the past you did some nasty things. Some people feel they've failed in some way. Others even discover that they've been murderers. It's important that these people understand that the very reason we come here is to explore every side of human nature, but that in the end there is a balance. Karma ensures that there is a balance. Therefore, guilt for attending the required 'classes' is nonsensical. Yet this emotion is the one that holds you back more than any other. It's the one most people have to deal with.

Acknowledging it and then dismissing it as historical records only, is the way to progress, and is the ultimate aim for all souls.

CHAPTER 14

The Fragmented Soul

Sometimes, following a traumatic death, especially from a lifetime that was full of unresolved issues, your soul can become fragmented. This means that you feel you are lacking in some area. Your soul has been split into two or more pieces. You don't feel complete and maybe you try all kinds of inappropriate partnerships, on a personal or a business level, to try and make yourself feel complete, and stumble from one business disaster or failure to another.

You may have a problem saying 'No' to people, or making decisions. You lack confidence and feel that your personality is too bland. If you feel this way, you might try all sorts of outlandish methods to make yourself more memorable to others, such as body piercing, tattoos and strange clothing. You're unable to assert yourself, or you feel a need to bully people to get your own way. You don't think they'll like you enough to do it just because you ask nicely.

*

I Left My Assertiveness Behind

Mandy had this problem. She had no ability to say 'No' at all, and had become a doormat for a succession of fair-weather friends and partners. People always did the same thing to her in the end. She would set no boundaries on new friendships, feeling that if she did people wouldn't be drawn to her. The problem was that the wrong people were drawn to her because of her compliant nature. They would act like friends, but only as long as she gave in to their every whim and demand. Eventually, they'd step over a boundary that was too far for her, putting on her so much, borrowing money and personal items, crashing in her home uninvited, until at last she would be forced to rebel. As soon as she did, they would turn on her, vilify her and leave her, alone again.

To rectify this fragmentation of her soul that made her lacking, she first had to be regressed. Mandy lives in the north-east and her past life was set in the south east. As with some people under hypnosis, her accent and her way of speaking were extremely different while she was speaking under hypnosis.

Mandy: *I'm in a big house in the county of Kent. It's the early winter of 1832. I feel heart-broken, torn apart, destroyed. My husband has gone. When he was first taken I was told that he was going to fight in the war, and that one day he'd return safe to me, but it was a lie. My parents lied to me. I've been betrayed by those who should love me. How could they do it? I know they've had him killed. I feel bereft.*

Later

It's night. I lie alone when I should have him in my arms. My skin is frigid where he should have warmed it. There's a storm brewing. It matches my feelings, which are dark and sinister. The wind howls in the chimneys like my heart howls in pain. I know he's cold and dead, and I don't want to live without my beloved.

Later

I stand at the edge of the cliffs, staring down at the wild sea below as it batters against the rocks. It's freezing cold this day, but I don't feel it. The dawn is rising on a new day, but I won't see it. The wind lifts me effortlessly and I float out into the buffeting wind. I must be falling, but I don't feel it. I seem to be floating down. Finally, I hit the water and then a part of me strives to live. My arms and legs thrash, but I stifle them. Within seconds they can move no more as the icy sea seeps into my bones. I sink...

*

Now we had recovered the place where the trauma happened. Not so much the death, but the emotional horror of being so badly betrayed. Mandy needed to visit the site to see if anything of herself remained there as a 'ghost'.

Sure enough we discovered that the house in question was reputed to be haunted by a young woman. Her ghost was seen walking from the house to the cliff edge, wailing all the way. The cliffs had eroded over the years, and so her spirit would walk on past the current edge, apparently out into space.

It seems to me that in most instances, ghosts are not complete entities. I'm not talking about the spirits that apparently come through from another realm, using mediums, and seem to be walking, talking, live beings that have come through from beyond to communicate with someone. I'm talking about the apparitions that seem to haunt various places, and are generally unwelcome, scaring the current occupiers. They are not fully visible, they don't speak, and drift around aimlessly with no apparent purpose. They don't seem to be incarnate spirits, who might be trapped here and looking for the light. And which of us would like to think that we could end up that way – our whole being condemned to wander around our old homes forever? I don't believe that's the case, and I don't believe ghosts are whole souls.

So, what are they and why are they there? Could they be who we were? I think that all these vaporous entities reported and photographed are actually a part of someone alive today, who could, like Mandy, benefit from returning to their old *haunts* and collecting that part of them that has been left behind. I feel this theory neatly ties up a lot of loose ends for me. I hope it does for you too.

*

Mandy: I never actually saw the ghost, but I do believe she was a part of me. It was an incredible experience. When I visited the house, I had several spontaneous flashbacks that told me more about my life there and the husband I loved and lost. But that wasn't the most amazing thing. I actually started to feel myself getting stronger as I walked the path to the cliffs. It really was as though I was collecting a facet of myself that had been left at that place, waiting for me to come back.

Since that day I have had no problems saying 'No' to people who would take advantage of me. I've cut out the dead wood from my life and have new friends. Nowadays when I make a new friend I put boundaries in right away. Unlike the old days, I don't give heart and soul to them right away, and I don't make myself available to their convenience. Nowadays trust takes time and respect has to be earned. They are better and truer friends for it.

Shell Shocks

Jerry lived in Northern Ireland. He grew up to the sound of gunfire and the occasional bomb. It was just a fact of life to him, and he never even jumped when the bangs tore through the air, even close to him. Nevertheless he felt 'dead inside'. He didn't feel he was capable of really loving anyone and had two failed marriages to prove it. He said whenever he tried to commit himself fully to a woman, he would find himself backing away, and his abiding thought was that he was not 'really a man' and didn't deserve a woman to love him.

Jerry: *Oh God, oh God. It stinks. The mud, the blood, vomit, all mixed together. Our feet and legs are caked with it. Tomorrow we go over the top for the second time. At dawn. It's what we came here for – to be heroes, but we never thought it would be like this. To die, shot like a dog, dying in the mud, alone. Yesterday, James was killed. Not outright. No one deserves to die like that, half his face shot away. He kept crying out for his Ma. My name is Jonny, that's what my mum calls me. I'm eighteen years old. God, I'll never see her again. I picture her getting the telegram and crying. Dad will put on a brave face, but he'll be crying inside. I almost want to get it over with. Might as well. I'm not getting out of here. My ears are ringing with bangs. I barely flinch anymore. I'm going numb. It's the only way to stay sane.*

Later

There's no sleeping. The noise is constant. They shot two boys this morning. They just broke down and tried to run. Shot by their own officers. Seems like we die here whatever, their bullets or ours, makes no difference, except ours are quicker. It's tempting. The last action we won, but most of us still died. Our guns that were meant to give us cover fell short and shells came down on us. That was when James got it. I held him, long as I could, but then I had to leave him and run. I left him to die out there alone. I feel sick.

Later

It's time. Boys in line are throwing up, retching. They didn't eat anything, but still they retch. I don't feel anything. I'm not scared. I'm refusing to think about anything bad. As I climb out of the trench I can see mum's garden. I'm just going to walk in the garden. If I see when I'm walking, I might find myself stepping on James' body. I can't smell anything but roses. I can't hear anything but the sound of angels singing. I see only the sun. So bright. So bright.

*

Jerry wasn't a coward but the awfulness of the situation surrounding his death, the total shock, and his shutting down in a feeble act of self-preservation, had left a terrible mark on him. He'd come back to a place of violence and bloodshed and shocking noise, just to try and prove to himself that he wasn't a coward. He deserved to find love and be loved, but his lack of ability to commit was due to the trauma of death that befell him and his companions in disgusting conditions on the battlefields of France. Today he is stronger. He has collected that part of poor Jonny that he'd left behind and I'm sure he'll soon regain a normal life and meet that special someone he can be happy with.

Jerry: This helped me so much. Healing started right away, but to make myself whole again, I had to go to the battlefield. I knew where I'd fallen as Jonny. I stood there among the memorials and wept. I wept for Jonny, for James, and for all the poor boys that had died there, for nothing. I sensed that part of me, a young, broken part, still remained near Jonny's body. I welcomed that facet of myself back, and then at last I felt peace. I wasn't a coward. I didn't have anything to prove.

CHAPTER 15

A Weighty Problem

You know that being overweight is bad for your health and your self-esteem, and you hate it, yet you can't stop over-eating. You like to look good, but every time you feel down, out comes your sugar fix, usually in the form of chocolate. You know all the old arguments about blood sugar highs and lows making you crave sugar, and you know they're all true, but food gives you a kind of comfort. It's not just the taste of sweet stuff with you, it's the notion that you *need* to eat. It's almost is if you're starving and you have an overwhelming compulsion to eat.

When willpower allows you diet madly, the weight goes, but just when you think it's safe to strip off in the open plan changing rooms in some shops, back comes the lack of confidence, out come the fatty or sugar-laden 'treats', and back comes the weight, more than ever. You're stuck on the yo-yo, going up and down, helplessly, and you just can't get off. You may even have been warned by your doctor of imminent diabetes or heart problems, but still your need to eat, to somehow fill your body and the void in your spirit, overtakes your fear of being ill.

*

Eating to survive

Amazingly, overeating can be because of a past life trauma, as in Jackie's case. She was a beautiful person, but it has to be said she would be even more beautiful (and healthier) if she could shed the three stone, 40 pounds, she constantly lost and regained – and keep it off. Each time losing it was getting harder and harder, and finally she decided to look to her past to see if she was self-destructing for some reason, or as I suspected, if she was actually carrying out self preservation.

Her regression gave us some answers.

Jackie: *My name is Gabrielle and I love to dress and live well. The year is 1924 and everyone I know feels we have to live as much as we can in case war comes to us as again, we fear it might. I'm American born, and I live in Paris. I have many beautiful gowns and shoes to die for, and I live to the full. Parties go on here night and day, and I love them. The cost of living is cheap here compared to back home and we all make the most of it.*

Later

I'm an artist, but independently wealthy. I think I have talent. I hope I have talent, and where else would an aspiring artist live but here in Paris, at this time? A major gallery has optioned my work. I'm so excited! Life is wonderful. The exhibition starts tonight. All my friends are coming. This will be the party of the century and the start of my real life. I never realized how much I wanted this until I started to believe it could happen. People are going to adore me, buy my paintings, and commissions from royalty are likely. I drink a gin and tonic while getting dressed in my most fabulous gown. I look fantastic. I'm the ideal clothes-horse, although some might say I'm a little bony, the clothes hang on me to perfection. Designers would almost pay me to wear their creations. I've got a new fur coat so I'm going to walk to the gallery. People in the streets will see me and wonder who I am. They'll soon know!

Walking was a mistake. I'm scared. Someone is following me. I shouldn't have worn my fine clothes, and the jewelry, why was I so vain? If he wants to rob me he can. I won't resist. I'm tempted to throw my rings and necklace onto the ground and run. There's another one! He's jumped out in front of me. A knife. No! No! I'll give them my jewels. The knife flashes and I feel nothing at first. Now a pain, hot and deadly. Then I'm suddenly growing cold, falling, fading...

Jackie: It was awful, such a sudden and violent death, and just as the good things in life were mine for the taking. What rotten timing! Everything was laid out like a map and then I got stabbed to death. Why couldn't they have just wounded me? Because I was so skinny, that's why! No wonder being skinny doesn't feel 'safe' to me.

The fact that Jackie died so quickly is what has lived with her. In this life it's holding her back in two ways. First, she's a bit afraid to be happy in case it's suddenly snatched away. Finding out why she fears that will happen should start her towards healing and letting herself live life to the full. Second, her weight is obviously something she wears like armor. She believes that if she's thin a knife will easily pierce vital organs, just like it did with Gabrielle. With all the padding she lays down she thinks maybe she could survive a knife attack.

Since understanding that this problem was in the past and not going to happen to her again, she has started to lose weight and keep it off.

*

Eating but Starving

Jock was the other end of the scale. He too was eating far too much to be healthy but he still felt the need to eat more. His biggest problem was that because he was a single dad and preparing his teenage kids' meals at different times of day to fit in with their lifestyles, he was constantly tempted to pick and finish up leftovers. He couldn't bear to tip any left over food into the bin, and would eat even things that were pretty disgusting or didn't even taste nice, such as cold, congealed eggs or sweet stuff mixed with gravy. Sometimes he'd mix it up deliberately to avoid being tempted, but food was food and if it was there he had to eat it.

Jock: *It's 1846. I'm wearing rags, with nothing on my feet. I'm Patrick. We've nothing to eat. The crop has failed, blighted, and yet still they send food to England. Mam cries herself to sleep at night and we do too. She cries because she can't feed us and we cry because of the pain in our bellies. I look at my sisters and their eyes are sunk into their heads. Their arms and legs are like sticks. I hope this is their last night and pray they don't wake up in the morning. I can't stand to hear them suffer; they cough as if they'd bring up their very lungs. Can there be a slower or worse way to die. It's so unfair. We worked so hard and have nothing for it.*

Later

The others went days ago. Dadda was the last to go. I think he thought I was dead too, but I was just too weak to move. They came for me, they finally came for me. Some charitable souls brought me soup and I could barely get it down. One sip at a time of the best thing I ever tasted. I'm going to survive at least for now, until sickness gets me too. If only they'd come sooner. I only lived because I didn't get sick like the others in my family. I was able to eat the last of our food when they were too weak.

Jock: I felt a bit guilty at having survived after my family had died, but I really couldn't have done anything else. I know I would have tried to help my family, but was too weak. I would have died anyway if those people hadn't come. I think I overeat now because my subconscious is frightened of me starving. I think now I know why, I'll be able to bring myself to bin that garbage.

Yes, Jock was eating because he was afraid of starving. His soul, made frugal by that dreadful experience, couldn't bear to see any scrap of food wasted. When you've lived in times when just a morsel of food could mean the difference between life and death, that feeling he had becomes understandable. Food shouldn't be wasted, and it's very tragic to know that there are *still* people starving in the world through no fault of their own, but there's certainly no need for Jock to eat himself to death.

*

CHAPTER 16

Your Child and Past Lives

Some of the best documented and well-proven incidences of past life recall have come from the testimony of children as young as two years old.

For instance the story of six-year-old James Leininger was reported on ABC's TV show Primetime in the USA, and it caused a huge response. As a two-year-old, James only ever wanted to play with toy planes. No cowboys, no soldiers or swords or pistols, just planes.

This kind of phenomena is called 'gathering the familiar'. It occurs when people feel unnaturally comfortable with artifacts from certain times or events, or in certain places. At the same age he started to have terrible nightmares, and he would wake up screaming, "Airplane crash on fire, little man can't get out," which was of course alarming for his parents. James was dreaming of being in a plane that was shot down.

James' mother Andrea, was first awoken to the possibility that the increasingly violent nightmares stemmed from a past life, by her own mother. She suggested that Andrea should get in touch with Carol Bowman, an expert on children's past life memories. In one video of James, taken at the time, he went over a toy plane as if he was giving it a pre-flight check. Another time Andrea bought James a toy plane, and pointed out what appeared to be a bomb on its underside. James corrected her, and told her it was a drop tank, which she had never heard of. It turned out that a drop tank was an extra petrol tank, which was strapped to the underside of the wings of an aircraft in WWII, to increase its flight range. Once empty it would be 'dropped'.

It was these incidents that prompted Andrea to talk to Carol

Bowman, despite her husband Bruce's skepticism, and Carol instructed her on how to question her son to discover if this was indeed a past life.

Once Andrea started having detailed conversations with James about his nightmares, they started to become less frequent, but he became able to talk about his past life while he was awake. This meant that details he came up with could be checked as facts. It was starting to look very convincing that this was indeed a past life.

James said that his plane had taken off from an aircraft carrier, which he named as the Natoma, and that he had flown a Corsair aircraft, with a man called Jack Larson. James complained that the Corsair was always getting flat tires. He said he had died in a plane that had been shot down by the Japanese.

Research showed that the Natoma Bay was in fact a small aircraft carrier in WWII, and that a man called Jack Larson had flown from it. However, the name 'Corsair' didn't seem to be right at the time, although it was known that they were prone to suffer flat tires on landing.

At that point James' sceptical father Bruce became obsessed with trying to disprove the past life theory, but everything he did just seemed to confirm it instead. James told him that he had been shot down at Iwo Jima, and labeled his drawings of himself as 'James 3'. To his amazement, Bruce discovered that not only had the ship been at Iwo Jima, but that the only pilot killed from the squadron that flew from it was James Huston Jnr. James also said that his plane had sustained a direct hit on the engine. Ralph Clarbour, a rear gunner on a U.S. airplane that flew off the Natoma Bay, says his plane was right next to one flown by James M. Huston Jr. during a raid near Iwo Jima on March 3, 1945. Clarbour said he saw Huston's plane struck by anti-aircraft fire. "*I would say he was hit head on, right in the middle of the engine,*" he said.

Bruce clung to the apparently incorrect fact that James had said he flew a Corsair, because Huston had been shot down in a FM2 Wildcat fighter plane, and there was no mention anywhere of Corsairs. This apparent inaccuracy gave him hope that everything was just a series of coincidences.

Just to make sure, Bruce tried to find members of Huston's family. In February of 2003 he made contact with Anne Huston Barron, Huston's sister, who now lives in Los Gatos, California. Through several phone conversations, they became friends, and she agreed to send Bruce photos of her brother during his military service. The packages of photos arrived in February and March of 2003.

In one of the packages was a photo of Huston standing in front of a Corsair fighter plane – the same kind of plane James had mentioned over and over. According to declassified U.S. military records, before Huston joined up with the Natoma Bay and VC-81, he was part of an elite special squadron, which test-flew Corsairs for carrier use.

When he learned this, Bruce says, all of his skepticism vanished. He is now totally convinced that his son had a past life in which he was James M. Huston Jr. Anne Barron believes it too, and calls him James 3, while James refers to the 86-year-old woman as his sister.

James' vivid recollections are starting to fade as he gets older, and this is what normally happens. However he is never far away from two of his most precious possessions, which his 'sister' Anne sent him; a bust of George Washington and a model of a Corsair aircraft. They were among the personal effects of James Huston, which were sent home to his family after the war.

James had three G.I. Joe dolls and called them Leon, Walter and Billie. According to U.S. Pacific Fleet records, Lt. Leon Stevens Conner, Ensign Walter John Devlin and Ensign Billie Rufus Peeler were among the fatalities from the Natoma Bay.

When asked why he gave the dolls those names, James

answered, "*Because they greeted me when I went to heaven.*"

*

Recognizing Your Children's Past Life Memories

There are several signs that would indicate your child is remembering a real past life, as opposed to merely exercising a fertile imagination:

1. The child won't use an excited tone of voice, but will speak of what they remember in a down to earth and relaxed way, just as if they were describing something that happened to them yesterday.

   My friend's son announced to his mother, while they were driving over a bridge in Kent, England, "Last time I drove over a bridge, I was a lady, and the car fell into the water and I died."

   To his mother's amazement she discovered that a woman had indeed crashed her car on the bridge and drowned when it fell into the deep river below. There is no logical reason why this boy should have said that he was a woman, or that he had died, except that it was a past life he was referring to.

2. If your child repeats the story many times, as they will do with real memories, it should remain consistent and details shouldn't vary. It's a good idea for that reason to make notes. Most children's memories fade as they reach around age seven, so it's good to have the notes anyway for your child's future reference.

3. If your child seems to have knowledge beyond his years, for instance playing complicated music from a very early age, or knowing how to assemble a carburetor or being able to paint, then these skills will very likely be something that's been

brought through from a previous lifetime.

4. If your child tells you that once he or she was injured or killed
   in a past life in a specific way, such as by bullet, they might
   well have a corresponding scar or birthmark relating to it. Or
   if they claim to have been a dog-handler in a previous life, see
   how dogs relate to them. If dogs are naturally respectful of the
   child and inclined to automatically treat them as pack leaders,
   then it's likely your child is right.

*

So, if you think your child has a genuine past life memory, what
should you do? The most important thing is not to scare the child
or make them think they're doing something strange or wrong.
Let them talk at their own pace and just interject with simple,
non-prompting questions if necessary, such as, "What were you
feeling at the time?" "What happened after that?" It's OK to ask
for details, such as, "Do you know how old you were then?" "Do
you know the year when that happened?" "Do you know what
your name was?"

If the child has said that they remember dying, like my
friend's son did, they probably won't be scared of the concept,
and this is a very good opportunity to stop them becoming afraid
of death later in life, so try not to be freaked out about it, and just
discuss it dispassionately.

A good question to ask to consolidate this natural feeling
about death is to ask them what happened afterwards. This will
bring the child the much-needed understanding that death is not
the end of their existence, and that is something everyone would
like to have total faith in.

Of course another reason that children's past life memories are
important is that the other people they claimed to have shared a

life with are often still alive. This means that facts can be corroborated. There have even been recorded cases where a mother has
found her children from her previous life, alive in this life. The
children accepted her proof that she had been their mother once,
even though she was now of course younger than they were.

*

Another fascinating subject when it comes to children's past lives
especially is xenoglossy, the ability to speak a language they have
not been taught. This is more common in children than in adults.
One child I know of spoke very strangely when he was first
learning to talk. It was to his parents as if he was speaking his own
made-up language. They soon recognized that when he said the
word, 'poto' he wanted a drink. They indulged what they thought
was his little idiosyncrasy, until one day a Greek-speaking friend
called round and told them that 'poto' was in fact Greek for
'drink'. It turned out that most of the little boy's 'made up
language', was also perfect Greek.

Xenoglossy is one of the greatest proofs offered for past life
memories, and gives skeptics the hardest time, whether encoun-
tered in children or adults. It discounts other commonly-used
dismissive evidence.

First you need to rule out telepathy, by testing. Next you have
to investigate the possibility of genetic (inherited) memory. For
instance, if you are born able to speak French, and yet you can
trace your family back for hundreds of years, until you go back
past the date of your memories, without encountering any French
blood, then you didn't inherit the memory from your ancestors. If
that's the case then this 'foreign' language has to come from a
genuine past life memory.

CHAPTER 17

How to Get There Safely

So you're convinced that delving into your own past might be a good idea and you want to know more. What happens exactly when you're regressed?

Do you worry about handing control of yourself over to someone else? Will you know what you're saying, or will you be unconscious, vulnerable, have ideas planted, be made to act like a chicken doing an Elvis impression? You don't need to worry about any of those things. Yes, you do have to take some care in selecting an experienced therapist who's going to take you on a safe journey, but it's not too hard to do.

To this end I have compiled what I believe could be the most comprehensive list of therapists in the world. They are listed at the back of this book and on my website: www.jennysmedley.com

Have a good look through them, visit their websites and choose one that resonates with you. It's better to travel some distance to reach the right person to help you. This is a very important spiritual journey you're about to take, so penny-pinching over the physical miles would be silly.

To answer your other questions, you won't be unconscious while hypnotized, and you will be aware of what you're saying. We're not talking entertainment here either, so no singing chickens. A therapist will hypnotize you. They will take you to a very quiet and relaxed state, so that your subconscious mind, which is normally drowned out by the mundane issues of life in general, will have a chance to come forward. Your subconscious has all your memories stored away, from every life you've lived, waiting for you to access them and unravel the skeins of your true self.

The therapist won't plant any ideas or feed you with any information. He or she will merely ask your subconscious questions and allow it to answer. The questions should always be open-ended. For instance: "Is anyone with you?" Rather than, "Who is with you?" The first allows your subconscious to answer freely either way, while the second makes your subconscious accept that someone *is* there.

*

One tip is to use my CD, or any of the other good past life CDs, before you try the real thing. This way you'll get some clues as to where you go in the regression, and this will save you time and money, as only one session with the therapist should be needed. These CDs are not meant as a substitute for regression with a therapist, but an extra tool. When you experience regression with a therapist guiding you, they'll be able to ask you specific questions, so you'll get much more information than you would just using a CD.

Another way, apart from using my list to find a therapist, is to go by personal recommendation. The caution is necessary because anyone can set themselves up as a regression therapist, even if they have never been trained in any way. The other thing that needs to be addressed is that a person can be a very experienced and competent hypnotist, and yet have very little or no experience of past life regression. You need to be with someone who has that knowledge, because the types of problems that can arise and need healing can be very different than the 'normal'. If someone you know has had a successful and life-shaping session with a therapist, then you can feel reasonably secure that you will too. So, what do you do if there is no recommendation available to you? You should ask your proposed therapist a few key questions. Don't be shy or afraid to ask questions. This could be the most important decision you've ever made after all. If a therapist isn't willing to be asked questions, then walk away and find one who is.

1. How much experience have you had of past life regression?

2. What safeguards will you put in, in case I am distressed by what I see?

3. How will you finish the regression and bring me out?

4. What will you do to heal my death in that lifetime?

5. What will you do to heal any traumas I remember?

6. What level will I reach?

The answers should be something on the lines of:

1. I have regressed many people, and have resolved their current life problems by exploring their past.

2. You will be able to come out of the session at any time if you want to. You'll be able to just ask me.

3. I will take you through your death in that life, so that the circle is completed.

4. I will bring you out to the light and let you look back and observe your body, so that you see that death is nothing to be feared.

5. I will talk you through the trauma and discuss with you

what you learned from it. I will make sure that the trauma is released and stays in the past, where it belongs.

6. I will make sure that you only reach the levels gradually, and that if you progress to Level 5, I will bring you back slowly through the levels, to make sure that you are fully detached from the past.

Failure to do these things leaves you open to becoming 'stuck' in that life, which has happened to me once. In my case, I believe it was necessary, but most people should avoid it.

There are many levels of trance too, from seeing just a flickering snapshot of your past, like a fuzzy television, right through to actually re-experiencing the past as vividly as you would if it was happening right now.

Level 1. This is not a very deep regression and you will only get glimpses of your past. As with most mediums' messages, the facts will be sketchy and you may well come out of the regression not quite sure if what you saw was real.

Level 2. In this level the picture will be very real, however, you will be viewing the events from a third party perspective, and the emotional involvement will only be a little stronger than if you were watching an emotive film. It will all seem very familiar to you, but you won't be quite sure if this was something that happened to you, or to someone else.

Level 3. At this level you will be aware of taking part in the events that unroll in front of you, and you may experience very empathic senses, such as taste and smell. The tale will seem a little surreal though, and may not be completely clear to you. There may be some confusion, and you might feel as if the person taking part is not really you. This, as in the previous level, is because your body, mind and soul are not quite re-united, and so that aspect of you which lived the life you are viewing, will still not feel quite like the real you.

Level 4. At this point all the emotions are very real, and will stay with you for the rest of your conscious lives. You will be very absorbed, and all the senses will be fully experienced. However, at this level you will still be peripherally aware of your current life and persona, and be aware that you are undergoing past life memories. The character in the events will be easily thought of as 'I', but you will still answer the therapists' questions, using references to your current life, such as 'I was older than I am now."

Level 5. This is as deep as you can get. You will be totally immersed in the past life, and have no awareness of your current life. You will answer questions in the present tense, such as, "I am walking down a narrow lane..." You will experience full detail and be aware of conversations, colours and moods. It is at this level that caution with choosing your therapist is vital. When I went for my first regression, it was totally unexpected to the therapist that I went straight to this level. As a consequence of inexperience I was brought out very quickly, and was still attached to that past life. Most people would need two or three sessions to reach this level. I don't believe I ever came fully back to the present, until I had a special healing session with Diane Egby Edwards.

*

Some people are afraid to be regressed in case they discover that they haven't had a past life as a human, and will then feel worse than they did before. Let me reassure you. If you are aware enough to ask the question, "Did I have a past life?" then you did indeed have one, and probably many. If someone has not experi-

enced any past lives they won't be reading this book and unlike
you, they won't have any spiritual depth.

*

So, you've decided to go ahead with this journey. You've chosen
a therapist who sounds experienced and suits your instincts. The
only thing that remains is for you to ask your guides and angels
to help you see what you're meant to see, feel what you're meant
to feel, and come away with a deep understanding of who you
really are.

If, under regression you come up with blocks, accept them,
because it's proof that your guides are doing what you asked
them to do. Trust that you'll find a clear path to the route you are
meant to take through your own history.

Not discovering who you really are will block your whole life this
time around. Imagine how tough it would be to live a fulfilled and
normal life if you were suddenly struck down with amnesia at age
40. You wouldn't know who to trust, you wouldn't remember
those loved ones who have always been there for you, and you
wouldn't recall the experiences that have structured your true
personality, so you'd lose all sense of self. To not recall past lives
is to continue in a state of spiritual amnesia of the soul, and it
makes life just as difficult as medical amnesia would do. Find out
who you really *are* by finding out who you really *were*.

Once you've succeeded in that, one of two things normally
happens. Either you'll have discovered what you came here to do,
which is often unfinished business from a past life, or the recalling
of a certain contract you made before coming here. Having a true
purpose to your life is what will make each of your days exciting,
challenging, meaningful and rewarding. Fulfilling that purpose or
that contract will make your life feel really free for the very first

time, and the rest of it will be spent productively and with contentment.

Or the experience will have opened you spiritually enough for a very important message to reach you. In my case an angelic visitation was next on the cards, and it was this angel who showed me my purpose in this life. This kind of message can show you a plan you would never have previously dreamed of, and probably wouldn't have believed if you hadn't been prepared by seeing your own past life.

Whichever path you are meant to tread as a result of finding out your own history, congratulate yourself for taking the first step and deciding to investigate yourself. This is the way to true happiness. Whether your goal in this life is to be a wonderful mother this time around, create a marvelous garden for wildlife, rekindle a lost love, climb a mountain that you once failed to climb, either metaphorically or factually, become a world leader, change the planet or create a special child, knowing which one, and concentrating on it, will show you *how to be happy*.

CHAPTER 18

Looking to the Future: Progression Therapy

Have you ever thought that glimpsing future lives might be instructive? That you might see the mistakes you're making in this life, and so find a way to avoid them in the next one, or even change what the next one is scheduled to be like?

I don't believe the future is set in stone, so 'progression' might just be a very good tool for figuring out what you're doing wrong, and changing your future.

This book is about being happy, so whatever might make you happy is a good thing. Of course unlike past lives there is no way of verifying these, but they do make sense, so who knows...

Women often have a lack of self-confidence, even in this day and age, so it was interesting to me as a past life consultant, to see if progression to a future life, might prove to be a successful therapy for them. 'Progression' is the complete opposite of 'regression', and takes you not into your own past lives, but into your future ones. The results were fascinating. Here are some examples:

Susan Arrowsmith

I had been a past life regressionist for over 20 years, and yet I had never managed to see one of my own past lives. I'd tried several times with other therapists. Something was blocking me, but what I hadn't realized was that the past wasn't where I needed to go. I don't know what finally gave me the nudge, but one of my students, Caroline, from the Anglia School of Hypnotherapy, had just completed her professional training as a hypnotherapist. We were spending a last afternoon at the school together.

"How do you feel about future life therapy?" she said. I trusted her, and something told me, look to the future... I found myself saying, "Yes, I'd like you to try and 'progress' me."

Part of me thought it was a silly idea, and I was sure I wouldn't get anything, or if I did, that it would be a meaningless jumble of nonsense. But what I actually saw converted me on the spot to the therapy of progression, and its validity in the field.

After taking me into a trance state, Caroline told me to make the leap from this life into my new body in a future life, and the first thing that happened to me was that I found myself in a male body. It took a few minutes to get used the feel of a man's anatomy – very weird. I looked down, and to my surprise I noticed I was wearing white, highly polished shiny shoes. But my feet looked larger than usual. My eyes traveled upwards and I was aware of the fact that I was dressed in a white lightweight suit of a fabric I had never seen before. In the same second I knew, without any doubt whatsoever that I was a man and my name was Brian McDonald.

Caroline's voice, traveling through time and space, broke into my thoughts and she asked me my name. My voice sounded strange and harsh to my own ears as I told her my name was Brian.

"How old are you Brian?"

"Thirty eight," I answered without hesitation.

"What year is it?"

"2280," I could hear myself say.

"Where are you Brian? Are you inside ...or are you out in the open?"

I looked around myself for the first time and noticed that I was at the controls of a vehicle, but it was not a car.

"I'm in the heli-mobile," I said, without thinking. Now how had I known that?

I was flying through the sky in something that was neither a plane nor a helicopter. In fact, as I looked at the screen in front of me I was aware of many similar craft around mine.

"I'm coming in to park," I said, aware that I was about to touch down on the top of a high-rise building.

"Where are you now Brian?"

Suddenly I knew all the answers, "I'm arriving at my office. This is where I work, and I'm in the city of London." I felt good as I landed my craft and a parked it. This was a place I knew well. An attendant opened the door for me. I didn't bother to acknowledge his greeting. This place was very familiar to me. I knew that I was an international broker in commodities. I had two offices, one in London and another in Brussels. I was extremely rich.

Suddenly Caroline's voice disturbed my thoughts, "Are you married Brian?"

"Oh yes, I'm married," I replied arrogantly. "I've been married for 18 years and I have two teenage daughters." Now where had that come from? I knew exactly what my wife looked like, small and pretty, with darkish hair and eyes. "Her name is Maura," I told Caroline.

"And your daughters?"

"Peta and Noreen," I replied, "They're twins."

"Do you enjoy family life?"

I knew we owned a large house in London, and also had a second home in Norway.

"Tell me where you are now Brian," Caroline said.

I looked round and saw that I was in a busy open plan office with very few people and large screens on several of the walls. This was the control point at which I bought and sold commodities in the world market place. Here I felt in control and very powerful, wheeling and dealing. I knew that I was very good at my job. I sat in a chair in front of one of the screens. The chair was so comfortable, as if my whole body was being supported in a completely different way than I am used to.

Eventually Caroline instructed me that it was time to make the leap back into the life that I had begun the session in, back into the body that I currently inhabited. I felt vaguely reluctant to leave. As Brian I had experienced emotions I had never experienced in my present life as a woman. I wanted to stay there in the year 2280 with Ireenie.

"Ireenie! Ireenie!" I shouted.

But it was too late. Caroline's voice was directing me to make the leap from my future life back into my body in my present life. It took me some moments to readjust to my normal wide-awake state. I would have to go forward again if I wanted to know who the mysterious Ireenie was.

"That was amazing," said Caroline. "You were so convincing."

"It was so real," I replied, "....and do you know something Caroline? It's just great being a man. Now I know what I've been missing all these years."

I was surprised that although I was a power man in a future life – and I found this an empowering experience to feel the strength of a strong man – that part of my future personality had similarities to this life. I had the same drive and motivation to wheel and deal in a future life as I do on a much smaller scale in this life as a woman. I'm looking forward to my future life.

*

Josephine

I'm quite well known as a psychic medium and healer. I believe that like most people I've lived many lives in the past and I was curious to discover if I was destined for a future life.

My therapist, Susan, guided me through the process of deep hypnosis to the point when I had the choice of making the leap from this life into a future one. I was feeling excited by the prospect and was able to give Susan the indication by raising my finger to let her know I was ready to leave my body in this life.

At first I felt disorientated and found that suddenly the language Susan spoke to me in was alien to me. It was as if Susan was speaking a foreign language and I had to try to translate it. I knew that my new name was strange and difficult to translate. I had the odd sensation that my facial features had changed and later Susan confirmed that my face had taken on an oriental appearance.

I understood and was able to tell Susan that I was a man in my future life, and extraordinarily, I was a space explorer. At the time I progressed to, I'd spent many years of exploration expeditions into deep outer space. My biological age was 34, but amazingly I felt I had lived much longer than that, as one of the good things about space exploration was that when traveling faster than light you don't age, but return home at the same age as you were when you began the venture.

On the downside I discovered that in my future life, I never married as this would be impossible when spending so many years away from the Earth, never knowing if I would return. However my new life was satisfying and rewarding and I wouldn't have chosen to have it any other way.

What I gained from the experience was the realization that the essential part of ourselves that we refer to as the soul, remains intact; despite the fact that I was a completely different person – and a man – my essential self remained unchanged. I found this comforting and it has reinforced my belief system of the soul passing from one life to another, unchanged.

Susan Arrowsmith is the founder of the Anglia School of Hypnotherapy and NLP and also the Anglia School of Psychic

Development.

She can be contacted on smarrowsmith@btconnect.com

If you wish to learn more about her courses visit her website: www.angliapsychics.com

*

Past Life Regression at Home

During the past four years, while I have been doing so many radio interviews and television appearances, talking about past lives, I have come to realize that so many people are fascinated by the subject. They are particularly interested in how it might impact on them personally. The problem is that constraints of time, money and to some extent fear, prevents many of them from seeking a professional therapist to lead them safely through the procedure.

I am also unable to spend the time doing one to one regressions any more, so I created a Past Life Meditation CD, which is designed to give people an alternative and safe way to dip into their past. I believe that once they have an inkling of what can be achieved this way, they will be encouraged to go for a full past life regression. This meditation CD can be used endless times, delving further and further into the past each time.

A lot of people also tell me that they are unable to reach meditative or hypnogogic states. This CD has been designed to help with that, and also should bring the person great improvements in their self-image, reduce their personal fears and give them a boost with their spiritual development in general, at the same time as giving them access to their own past lives.

Therapists

The inclusion of a therapist in this list does not mean the author always has personal knowledge or endorses every therapist. Prospective clients should always satisfy themselves of any particular therapist's credentials before consulting with them.

Almost all therapists listed have given their permission to be included. However, this does not mean they endorse all of the author's beliefs.

BRITAIN & EUROPE

ENGLAND

Carol Bowman
Children's past life expert
Website: http://www.childpastlives.com

Andrew Hillsdon
Devon / Cornwall
Chairman of The Past Life Therapists Association
Tel: 01409 211559
Email: info@pastliferegression.co.uk
Website: www.pastliferegression.co.uk

Sue Tribe
Clinical Hypnotherapist and Shamanic Healer
Dip. Clinical Hypnotherapy Dip. Past Life Regression Dip.
Spiritual Regression
The Grange Clinic, Private Road, Nottingham NG5 4DD.
MobILE: 07870 213456
Email: suetribe@ntlworld.com
Website: www.nottinghamhypnotherapy.co.uk

Rachel Keene
Stratton near Bude, Cornwall
Tel: 0845 833 0768
Email: rachelkeene@btinternet.com
Website: www.rachelkeene.net

Barbara Ford-Hammond
Alton, Hampshire
Tel: 44 (0)1420 588619
Email: barb@barbaraford-hammond.com
Website: www.barbaraford-hammond.com
and www.lomburlesque.com

Susan Arrowsmith
Principal of Anglia School of Hypnotherapy and NLP
46 Porter Road, Long Stratton, Norwich NR15 2TY
Tel: 01508 530926
Website: www.ash04.co.uk

Judy Hubbard
member of the Past Life Therapists Association
Worcester
Tel: 01905 622164
Email: hubbardj@btopenworld.com

Christina Elvin
Past Life Therapist
Northampton, England NN4 0RF
Tel: +44(0)1604 768343
Email: christina@emofree.biz
Website: www.emofree.biz

Michelle Simmonds.
Vauxhall, London SW8 2JB and the south west

Tel: 0207 582 4604
Email: michelle500simmonds@googlemail.com

Dr Michael G Millett
Elevated Therapy International
London NW
Tel: 0845 65 88 22 0
Website: www.pastlifehealing.co.uk

Dave Laing
Liverpool
Tel: 0151 931 4391
Email: hypno@davelaing.co.uk
Website: www.davelaing.co.uk/hypno

Maureen Jackson
12 Overton Road, Oakwood, London, N14 4SY
Tel: 0208 360 7019
Email: maureen-jackson@tiscali.co.uk
Website: www.maureenjackson.co.uk

David Holmes
North East England
Tel: 0191 237 5221
Website: www.davidholmeshypnosis.co.uk
Email: info@davidholmeshypnosis.co.uk

Tania Cheslaw
Cambridge
Tel: 0845 257 3021
Email: tanche_hyp@yahoo.co.uk
Website: www.taniacheslaw.co.uk

Nick Davies
Hypnotherapy NLP and Life Coaching
Coundon, Coventry, West Midlands
Tel: 024 7667 5520
Website: www.NDHypnotherapy.com

Diane Egby D.H.P.
Hypnotherapist / Sound Healer
Bournemouth
Tel: 01202 423111
Email: postmaster@hypnosounds.plus.com
Website: www.degby.wetpaint.com

Brenda White
Newark
Tel: 01636 677725
Email: bwhite@uk-therapists.net
Website:
http://www.bwhite.uk-therapists.net/past_life_therapy.htm

John Lenihan
Weston Super Mare, Somerset, BS23 2QQ
Tel: 01934-424261
Email: j297561@aol.com

Julie Winstanley – Warrington
Tel: 01925 422939
Email: julie@therapy4all.com

Dave Goodfellow
MNSPH. LNCP. SQHP
Clinical Hypnotherapist, Hypnoanalyist, Past Life Regression
Therapist
Boroughbridge, North Yorkshire

Tel: 01423 322325
Website: www.hypno-therapists.co.uk
Email: dave@hypno-therapists.co.uk

Barrie Anson
Hypnotherapy, Homeopathy, Nutritional Therapy
(Dorset, Somerset, Hampshire)
Rowan House, Malherbie Court, Knowle St. Giles, Chard,
Somerset TA20 4AZ
Telephone 01460 632380
Email: barrieanson@tiscali.co.uk

Frances Free
Hypnotherapist, Counsellor and Reiki Master
High Wycombe, Bucks
Tel: 01494 538832/07766 860867
Email:
frances_free@hotmail.co.uk
Website: www.hypnotherapyhighwycombe.co.uk

Barbara Lewis
(BN.Cs.(Hons) Psych. Cert Ed. CELTA, D.C.H. LCTTH (Dip)
MBSCH)
27 Priory Road, Dartford, Kent, DA1 2BL
Tel: 01322 285 678
Mobile:07930 301 581

Ruth Patience
DipCH: MPNLP.
Sandhurst, Berkshire
Tel: 01344 772084
Website: www.thepatienceclinic.com
Email: ruth@thepatienceclinic.com

Crystal Heart
Colchester, Essex
Tel: 01206 38159
Email: c.heart@btinternet.com

Angela Noon,
East Grinstead, Surrey/Sussex border
Tel: 01342 718357
Email: amnoon@dsl.pipex.com
Website: www.angelanoon.co.uk

Steve Burgess
Hypnotherapy and Emotional Freedom Technique /EFT
Beverley, East Yorkshire
Tel: 01482 870874
Email: steve@naturaltherapy.karoo.co.uk
Website: www.steveburgesshypnosis.com

Martina Rutherford
Dip Hyp, Dip CP, Dip PLT&SRT
Hypnotherapist, Past Life Regression, Spirit Release Therapist,
Tarot reader, and Reiki Healer
Hove, East Sussex
Tel: 01273 723963
Email: martina@holisticsoul.co.uk
Website: www.holisticsoul.co.uk

Judith Stone
South Yorkshire/Derbyshire
Tel: 01246 419038
Website: www.uncommon-practice.org.uk
Email: jude.stone@btopenworld.com

Moira Fitzsimmons
Birmingham
Tel: 0121 477 7067
Email: moira@litehouse.me.uk
Website: http://www.litehouse.info/

Margaret Pett
Dunstable
Tel: 01582 664733
Email: MagentaMOD123@AOL.com

Graham Howes
7 Harley Street London W1; also in Essex; Suffolk; Colchester
and Ipswich.
Tel: 01206 391050
Mobile: 07960 755626
Email: info@edgehypno.com
Website: http://www.edgehypno.com/page001.html

Douglas Craddock
Manchester
Tel 0161 282 9291 or 0161 881 7171
Email: hypnosis@karma7.supanet.com

Jeanette Sitton
D.Hyp.(Dist), LNCP
London
Riverside Private School of Complementary Therapies
Tel: 0208 376 8088
Email: info@riverside-workshops.co.uk
Web: www.riverside-workshops.co.uk

Anne Thornton-Patterson
London and Staffordshire

Tel: 0208 964 8591
Email: anne@kensingtonhypnosis.co.uk
Website: www.kensingtonhypnosis.co.uk

Niki Cassar
Cobham, Surrey
Tel: 01932 868 787
Mobile: 07973 346 747
Email: mail@nikicassar.com
Website: www.nikicassar.com

Foszia Turner-Stylianou
Kingston, Surbiton, Surrey
Tel: 0208 390 4995
Mobile: 247796
Email: foszia@tranceformingself.co.uk

NORTHERN IRELAND

Deena Craig
Bangor
Tel: 02891 458161
 Mobile: 0786769 7021
Email: deenacraig@freeuk.com
Website: http://www.hypnotherapistuk.com

SCOTLAND

Johan MacIver
Glasgow
The Wight Relaxation Clinic, 116 Elderslie Street, Charing Cross,
Glasgow G3 7AW
Tel: 07984 428 741
Website: www.wightrelax.co.uk

Karen de Jager
Aberdeen or home visits
33 Sumburgh Crescent, Sheddocksley, Aberdeen, AB16 6WG
Tel- 01224 636378- Mob- 07733 113138
Websites: www.takurei.com
www.pastliferegression.co.uk

Stan Gerard
Aberdeen
Tel: 01224 213 808
Email: stan.gerard@whsmithnet.co.uk
Website: http://users.whsmithnet.co.uk/stan.gerard/

Carolyn Clark Day
Edinburgh
Tel: 0131 557 6588
Email: Carolyn@karmafix.com
Website: www.karmafix.co.uk

WALES

Simon Childs
Rosedene Cottage, Llwyncelyn, Aberaeron, Ceredigion SA46
0HF
Tel: 01545 580368
Mobile: 07779 65871
Email hypnopastlives@yahoo.co.uk

Sue Stewart
Rhyl, North Wales
Tel: 01745 369616
Website:
www.hypnotherapy-regression.co.uk
E-mail: info@hypnotherapy-regression.co.uk

Ken Timmins
MSc Dip hyp, GQHP
Cardiff and Vale Hypnotherapy
Castle Court, 6 Cathedral Road, Cardiff, CF11 9LJ
Tel: 02920 647508
Mobile: 0772 330 5990
Email: sw.hypnosis@yahoo.co.uk
Website: www.sw-hypnosis.co.uk

Louise Hutchings
Dip,Hyp, FMCHTA, DPLT, MPLTA, EFT-CC
Ceredigion, Wales
Tel: 0845 2269345
Website: www.regress.me.uk

Meirion Ellis
HPD, DipCAH Clinical Hypnotherapist and Regression
Therapist
Chester, NW England; and Wrexham and Mold, North Wales
Tel: 0845 123 2954
Website: www.previouslife.co.uk

Cerys Evans
Iama Holistic Health and Well Being
Swansea
Email: cerys@iamaremedies.co.uk

IRELAND

Patrick J Dillane
Cottage Retreat, Coolbagh, Clashmore, Co Waterford
Tel: 00 35 3 24 96979
Email: patdillane@msn.com
Website: www.cottageretreat.net

Margaret Haire
Member of the Irish Council of Hypnotherapy/Psychotherapy
7 Holborn Hill, Belturbet, Co Cavan
Tel: 0 49 9524855
Email: mhaire@eircom.net

Fiona Shields
Angel Therapies, Killin, Bridge-a-Crinn, Dundalk, Co Louth
Email: fiona@angeltherapies.com
Mobile: 0872250146
Website: www.angeltherapies.com

Kathy Gibbons
Dublin
Tel: 01 6683774
Email: k.gibbons@orange.fr

CHANNEL ISLANDS

Azlanna Coote
DPLT MPLTA
Soul to Soul Therapy Center, 11 New Street, St Helier, Jersey,
JE3 1FR
Tel: +44 (0)1534 619323

AUSTRIA

Ursula Demarmels
Mattsee, Salzburg, Lake District
German, Swiss-German, English speaking
Website: http://www.spiritualregression.de

BELGIUM

Sky Hugman
Tel: 0405 683 345

FRANCE

Angela Noon
East Grinstead, Surrey/Sussex, England
and France, near Parthenay, Deux Sevres, Poitou Charentes
Tel: +44 (0)1342 718357
Email: amnoon@dsl.pipex.com
Website: www.angelanoon.co.uk

Kathy Gibbons
Dublin, Ireland, and Auxerre, France
Tel: 0608338992
Email: k.gibbons@orange.fr

GERMANY

Ulf Parczyk
Psychologist, Esoteric Psychology
Philipp-Puth-Str. 16, 60388 Frankfurt
Tel: ++49 (0) 61 09 / 50 84 30
Fax: ++49 (0) 61 09 / 50 84 31
Email: info@esopsych.de
Website: www.esopsych.de

Sigrid Westermann
Hamburg
Tel: 00 49 40 41 05 684
Email: info@lifeconcepts.de
Website: www.lifeconcepts.de

Christoph Graf von Keyserlingk
Louisenstr. 9 D 01099 Dresden
Tel: 00 49 (0)351 80 15 554
Email: ckeyserlingk@gmx.net
Website: www.reiki-zentrum-dresden.de

Inga Bucolo-Trappen,
Psychologist, Neuss near Cologne
Tel: 00 49 21 31 20 68 332
Email: praxis@bucolo-trappen.de
Website: www.bucolo-trappen.de

GREECE

Carolyn Clark Day
Edinburgh and Greece
Tel: 0131 557 6588
Email: Carolyn@karmafix.com
Website: www.karmafix.co.uk

ITALY

Allison Lee Axinn
Pietrasanta, Tuscany, Italia
Regression sessions are held at the Qion Center, via Barsanti 44,
Pietrasanta
Tel: (0039) 348 035 3737.
Email: a.axinn@tiscali.it
Website: http://www.qion.it/

Carolyn Clark Day
Edinburgh and Italy
Tel: 0131 557 6588
Email: Carolyn@karmafix.com

Website: www.karmafix.co.uk

NETHERLANDS

Anita Groenendijk
Wageningen, Netherlands, and near Germany
Tel: 00 31 317 425251
Email: info@pastlifetherapy.eu
Website: www.pastlifetherapy.eu

Marion Boon
IPARRT PRACTICE
PO Box 83, 3220AB, Hellevoetsluis, Netherlands
Tel: 00 31 181 322050
Email: marion@iparrt.nl
Website: www.iparrt.nl

Jon RG (Formerly Jon-Richard)
& Troya GN Turner
Grootebroek
Tel: 00 31 228 513 630
Email: Whole-Self@qicknet.nl
Website: www.Whole-Self.co.uk
Whole-Self.info

Kees Reijn
Hilversum
Tel: 0654 625429
Email: keesreijn@kredo.nl
Website: http://www.keesreijn.kredo.nl/

PORTUGAL

Maria Reboredo
Lisboa/ Portugal
Tel: 35 1 21 301 0725
Email: f.reboredo@netcabo.pt

Sueli Simões
MD, Vila Nova de Gaia, Porto
Tel: (+35 1) 96 907 0708
Email: suelisimoes@sapo.pt
Website: http://suelisimoes.blogs.sapo.pt

Alice Cabral
Lisbon
Tel. (00 35 1) 21 794 2185
Email: psicomundi@gmail.com

SPAIN

Robert Hutt
The Healing Therapy Centre,
Passatge Des Porxo 3, 07184, Calvia, Mallorca, Isles Baleares,
Spain.
Tel: 00 34 971 670 366
Email: robhutt@yahoo.com

Maria Gemma Saenz
TRCD
Plaza Joaquín Pena, 1 08017 Barcelona
Tel: 00 34 932 800 016
Websites: www.mariagemma.com
www.trcdamun.com

SLOVENIA

Dr Jan Erik Sigdell
Dutovlje
Tel: ++38 6 (0)5 764 04 67
Email: janeriksigdell@siol.net
Website: www.christian-reincarnation.com

SWEDEN

Jörgen Sundvall
Hypnoanalyst and Past Life Therapist
Gränna
Tel: +46 39 01 2288
Email: jorgen@sseah.se
Website: www.sseah.se

Berndt Nilsson
Valdemarsvik
Tel: +46 123 124 34
Email: mail@regression.nu
Website: www.regression.nu

Emine Karakaya
Stockholm
Tel: +44 (0) 79 8847 3558
Website: www.plr-emine.com
Email: emine100@hotmail.com

SWITZERLAND

Barbara Frey
Eglisau, Zürich
Tel.: 00 41 44 867 33 71

Email: barbara_frey04@yahoo.com

TURKEY

Diba Ayten Yilmaz
Istanbul
Tel: +90 532 274 44 70
Email: diba@radianced.com
Website: http://www.radianced.com

RUSSIA

Maria Volchenko
Moscow
Email: socol@orc.ru
 Website: http://www.dream-art.ru

Valentina Chupiatova
Moscow
Tel: 8 916 844 3477

Pavel Gyngazov
Tomsk
Email: 4749@mail.tomsknet.ru
Website: http://pastlife.tsk.ru

AUSTRALASIA

AUSTRALIA

Hitomi Akamatsu
Clayton, Victoria
Tel: +61 416 300 814
Tel: + 61 3 990 52799

Email: hitomi.akamatsu@education.monash.edu.au
Website: www.thetahealing.jp

Dr Frank Jockel PhD
Victoria
Tel: +61 39 885 0440
Email: frank@thefutureis.com
Website: www.thefutureis.com

Maggie Sinton
Canningvale
Tel: 93 51 9346
Fax: 93 51 9346

Verena Cunningham
Email: russnlp@pacific.net.au

Susan Friday
Melbourne
Email: susan@healing.at
Website: http://www.healing.at/

Michelle Mayur
Victoria
Tel: 03 98 88 0138
Fax: 03 98 08 3315
Website: http://www.angelwings-healing.com

Ruth Camden
Chatswood, New South Wales
Tel: (02) 94 15 2767

NEW ZEALAND

Anna Duggan
Dip CHT Clinical and Transpersonal Hypnotherapist
The Wellbeing Clinic, 2b O'Leary's Paddock, Sunshine Bay,
Queenstown 9300
Tel: +64 (0) 3 4413550
Mobile: +64 (0) 21 4713838
Email: thewellbeingclinic@xtra.co.nz

Bert Esser
Tauranga
Tel: 064 7 5442808
Email: bert.esser@ xtra.co.nz

NORTH AMERICA

CANADA

Thelma Beam
Toronto
Tel: 416 924 7215 X2
Email: ccr@pathcom.com
Website: www.mindmeldconsulting.com
and www.lawsofthejungledating.com

Karen Eardley
Toronto
Email: karrie@vianet.on.ca
Website: http://www.torontohypnotherapy.ca/index.html

Karen Eardley
Muskoka
Email: karen@muskokahypnotherapy.ca

Website: www.muskokahypnotherapy.ca

Rifa Hodgson
Vancouver/Sunshine Coast, BC
Tel: 604 741 7944
Email: rifa@lifebetweenlives.ca
Website: wwww.lifebetweenlives.ca

Georgina Cannon
D.Mc. BCH.
Toronto, Ontario
Tel: 416 489 0333
Email: georgina@ontariohypnosiscentre.com
Website: www.ontariohypnosiscentre.com

USA

Alabama

Sally Beth MacMaster PhD
Florida Panhandle, Southern Alabama
Tel: 407 712 3397
Email: drmacmaster@alternativechoice.net
Website: www.alternativechoice.net

Alaska

Jan Hardy
Anchorage
Tel: 907 868 8050/1250
 Email: NewRealities@alaska.com
 Website: www.WhiteSwanProductions.com

Jodi K. Carlson PhD

CCHT, HC
Tel: 907 232 1707

Arizona

Ashley Mann
Center for the Healing Arts, Tucson, Arizona
Tel: 520 241 1010
Email: ashleymann@yahoo.com
Website: http://myspace.com/ashleys_secret10

Linda S Novoa
CHt , LBLt
Glendale, Arizona
Tel: 623 505 3168
Email: novoa2novoa@cox.net
Website: www.tranquiltransitions.org

Dorothy M. Neddermeyer PhD
Phoenix, Arizona
Tel: 480 704 0603
Email: DorothyNed@gmail.com
Website: www.gen-assist.com
or www.drdorothy.net

Sandra Phocas
Tucson, Arizona
Tel: 520 705 1144
Email: info@experienceSacredHealing.com
Website: www.experienceSacredHealing.com

Nirup Barnum
Sedona
Tel: 928 203 0749

Email: Readings@PsychicNirup.com
Website: http://www.psychicnirup.com

California

Kathy Bornino
Arroyo Grande, California (south of San Luis Obispo)
Tel (805) 481 1724
email kbornino@yahoo.com

Peter Wright
Insights from Within
2335 Sonora Drive, Santa Barbara, CA 93105
Tel: (805) 682 6901
Email: pqwright@aol.com
Website: www.insightsfromwithin.com

Lucy Baker
San Francisco
Email: luce@iprimus.com.au
Website: www.lucybaker.net

Ann C. Barham
Gilroy
Tel: 408 930 0052
Fax: 408 847 5877
Email: acbarham@garlic.com
Website: http://www.pastlives.org/

Colorado

Greg McHugh CCHT
PO Box 100067, Denver, Colorado 80250
Tel: 1 303 995 4276

Email: gregmchughcht@earthlink.net
Website: http://www.gregmchugh.com

Connecticut

Dr Eilis Philpott
Connecticut
Tel: 203 372 6551
Email: eilis@soul2soulangelichealing.com
Website: www.soul2soulangelichealing.com

Patty Hall
Niantic
Tel: 860 439 0144
Email: pattyhall@sbcglobal.net
Website: http://www.thesourceoflight.com

Delaware

Rev. Angela J. Rapalyea
Tel: 215 233 0825

Florida

Rev. Marcy Roban
Ft. Lauderdale
Tel: 954 302 3059
Email: info@marcyroban.com
Website: www.marcyroban.com
and www.OneWorldMovement.org

Carin Friedman, MSW, LCSW
Sarasota
Tel: 941 365 4308

Email: carinfriedman@comcast.net

Georgia

Paul W. Schenk, Psy.D.
3589 Habersham at Northlake, Tucker, Georgia 30084-4009
Tel: office: 770 939 4473
Tel: toll free: 1-888-748-6823
Email: drpaulschenk@earthlink.net
Website: www.drpaulschenk.com

Idaho

Caren Seabeneck
Boise
Tel: (208) 378 9179
E-mail us: ihatt@msn.com
Website: http://www.innovativehealingarts.com

Iowa

Terry E. Gahm
Tel: toll free: 877-497-6747 or 402-896-3181
Email: Hypnosis@tconl.com
Websites: www.XPHypnosis.com
and www.HypnosisSuccess.com

Illinois

Susan Wisehart, M.S., LMFT
suburb of Chicago
Tel: 847 438 7878
Email: susan@susanwisehart.com
Website: www.susanwisehart.com

Kansas

Anne Brewer
Prairie Village
Tel: 1 913 722 5498
Email: info@annebrewer.com
Website: http://www.annebrewer.com

Kentucky

Samantha Doane-Bates
Tel: 859 224 0166
Email: sdoanebates@aol.com
Website: www.samanthadoane-bates.com

Louisiana

Dr. Vikki Ashley
New Orleans LA 70115
Tel: 504 895 7968
Fax:: 504 891 0864
Email: drvashley@bellsouth.net
Website: www.bitchwithstyle.com

Maryland

Janet Cunningham, Ph.D
Columbia, Maryland
Tel: 410 404 2997
Email: info@janetcunningham.com
Website: www.JanetCunningham.com

Helene N. Guttman, PhD
Bethesda, Maryland
Email: hguttman@soundbalance.net

Website: www.soundbalance.net

Massachusetts

Carol McGlinchey
Great Barrington, Massachusetts
Tel: 413 274 0286
Email: pastlife@roadrunner.com
Website: www.yourinfinitequest.com

Katrina Gannon Valenzuela
Barnstable
Tel: 508 362 7474
Email: transform999@aol.com
Website: www.transformationscenter.com

Minnesota

Kevin D. Doheny
Eagan, Minnesota
Tel: 651 688 2469
Email: kevin@soundmindbodyhealing.com
Website: www.soundmindbodyhealing.com

Missouri

Roger G. Literski
Hazelwood, Missouri (20 miles from St. Louis)
Email: northcountyhypnosiscenter@hotmail.com
Tel: 314 731 4515

Nebraska

Terry E. Gahm - Douglas

Tel: toll free: 877-497-6747 or 402-896-3181
Email: Hypnosis@tconl.com
Websites: www.XPHypnosis.com
and www.HypnosisSuccess.com

Nevada

Dr Tish Morgan
Las Vegas, Nevada
Tel: 702 456 3128 or 702 392 8392
Email: drtish7@aol.com
Website: www.drtish.org

New Jersey

Mark Sullivan
Tel: 609-713-2785

New York

Laurie Greenberg, Ph.D.
Clinical Psychologist
New York, New York
Tel: (212) 501 3707
Email: DrLGreenberg@aol.com
Website: www.soulcenteredtherapy.com

North Carolina

Vickie Penninger
Raleigh
Tel: (919) 828 0876
Email: vickpenn@bellsouth.net
Website: http://www.thereikichannel.com/

John Williams
Asheville
Tel: 828 626 4300

Ohio

Donna Nowak
Tel: 216 321 9181
Email: donna@DonnaNowak.com
Website: www.DonnaNowak.com

Oklahoma

Carol Lovato
117 W. Main Street, Watonga, OK 73772
Email: desperados@mail2.pldi.net

Oregon

Linda Carnemolla
Portland
Tel: 503 490 1632
Email: Hypnosiswithlinda@yahoo.com

Joelle McGonagle
Portland
Tel: (509) 427 3619
Email: Joelle@gorge.net.
Website: http://inner-light-counseling.com/

Pennsylvania

Barbara Kauffman
Astoria, Oregon and Berwyn, Pennsylvania

Tel: 503 325 1902
Email: barbara@auriclights.net
Website: www.auriclights.net

Rhode Island

Patti Towhill
Tel: 401 539 3353
Email: pattitowhill@gmail.com
Website: www.pattitowhill.com

Tennessee

Center for Peace, Seymour
Phone: 865 428 3070
Fax: 865 429 0842
Email: perry@centerforpeace.us

Texas

Shelley Kaehr
Dallas, Texas
Tel: (469) 556 4325
Email: shelley@shelleykaehr.com
Website: www.shelleykaehr.com

Eric B. Richmond, BCH, CI
Dallas
Tel: 214 356 3922
Email: eric@dallashypnosisconsultants.com
Website: www.dallashypnosisconsultants.com

Lois J. Wetzel
Houston

Tel: 713 334 5486
Email: lois@hotpinklotus.com
Website:
http://hotpinklotus.com/index.cfm/MenuItemID/113.htm

Petrene Soames
The Woodlands
Tel: (281) 363 9983
Email: information@petrene.com
Website: http://timeismine.com

Vermont

Betty Moore-Hafter
Burlington, Vermont
Tel: 802 860 7286
Email: betty@risingsunhealing.com
Website: www.holistichypnotherapyeft.com

Virginia

Kelly DeMarce, CH, RMT
Certified Hypnotherapist, Reiki Master / Teacher
Herndon
Tel: 703 371 9820
Email: hypnosoul@hotmail.com
Website: www.hypnosoul.net

Scott Gauthier
Charlottesville
Phone: 434 760 5999 or 540 456 8639
Email: scott@awarebody.com
Website: http://www.awarebody.com

Washington

Mary Lee LaBay
Bellevue, Washington
Tel: 425 562 7277
Email: marylee@maryleelabay.com
Website: www.maryleelabay.com
and www.AwarenessEngineering.com

Wisconsin

Susan Wasserman
Shorewood
Tel: 414-961-0649
Email: info@inrjourneys.com
Website: http://www.inrjourneys.com/index.htm

Nancy Hornby
Shorewood
Tel: 414 332 8159
Email: info@inrjourneys.com
Website: http://www.inrjourneys.com/index.htm

CARIBBEAN/CENTRAL /SOUTH AMERICA

CARIBBEAN

Diana Bourel
St Barthelemy
Tel: 590 590 27 98 10

BRAZIL

Elaine Gubeissi De Lucca

Sao Paulo
Tel: 011 212 6419

EQUADOR

Mehra Atul Kumar
Tel: 593 9 733 940

MEXICO

Angelina Ahumada Rodríguez
Insurgentes Sur 2376-104
Col. Chimalistac
Tel: (55) 56 16 91 56
Email: altern@prodigy.net.mx
Website: www.alternativamexico.com

AFRICA

SOUTH AFRICA

Kim Morris
Randpark Ridge, Johannesburg, Gauteng, South Africa
Tel: +27 11 82 653 8419
Website: www.soulconnection.co.za
Email: kim@soulconnection.co.za

Jacques Theron
Cape Town
Tel work: 00 27 21 439 5041
Mobile: 00 27 82 817 5266
Email: inspire@telkomsa.net
Web: www.inspire-network.com

INDIA

Vijay Jain
Gujarat
Tel: 91 079 26 75 1010
Email: vijayhealing@yahoo.co.in
Website: http://www.geocities.com/vijayhealing/vijay.html

FAR EAST / MIDDLE EAST

CHINA

Yasemin Tokatli
Shanghai
Email: tiamatian@mail.com
Website: http://www.earth-association.org/

Tammie Meijer
Mobile: 00971 50 4296 107
Email: tammie_meijer@hotmail.com

ISRAEL

Georgina Johnson
Tel: 972 04 639 2396
Email: veratherapy@yahoo.com
http://www.geocities.com/veratherapy

Brigette Kashtan
Haifa
Phone: 972 4 825 1020
Fax: 972 4 824 2660
Email: bkashtan@netvision.net.il

website: Brigitte-Kashtan.com

MALAYSIA

Vivienne Leong
Tel: 6019 3317 452

Selina Chew
Selangor
Tel: (+6)013-6302926
Email: selina@life-inspirations.com
selina@life-inspirations.com
Website: http://www.hypnosissolutions4u.com/index.html

SEYCHELLES

Barry Laine
Transform-therapies (Sey), The Wishing Well Clinic,
Anse Des Genets, Mahe, Seychelles
Tel/ Fax: 00248 374477
Mobile: 00248 515616
Email: barrylaine@transform-therapies.sc
Website: www.transform-therapies.sc

SINGAPORE

Poonam Uppal
Omrit Healing Centre
Email: poonam@poonamuppal.net
Website: http://www.poonamuppal.net/index.html

Chantal Brosens
Email: reconnectwithin@yahoo.com.sg

B O O K S

O books
O is a symbol of the world, of oneness and unity. In
different cultures it also means the "eye", symbolizing
knowledge and insight, and in Old English it means "place
of love or home". O books explores the many paths of
understanding which different traditions have developed
down the ages, particularly those today that express
respect for the planet and all of life.

For more information on the full list of over 300 titles
please visit our website
www.O-books.net

SOME RECENT O BOOKS

The Night of the Unicorn
Jenny Smedley

Jenny and Tony Smedley have created an enchanting world with a beautiful and positive message. This book contains a wonderful, spiritual tale which is perfect for today's more sophisticated young reader. A breathtaking bedtime read, that neither you nor your child will want to put down. **Jacky Newcomb** Psy.D, *Sunday Times* best selling author of *An Angel Saved My Life*

9781846940347 160pp **£7.99 $14.95**

Forever Faithful
Dogs That Return
Jenny Smedley

Enchanting. Jenny's true-live(s) story of her beloved dog and horse are a must read for every person who has ever loved, and been loved, by an animal companion. **Rae Ann Kumelos**, Voice of the Animal

978-1-84694-174-0 160pp **£9.99 $19.95**

Striking at the Roots
A Practical Guide to Animal Activism
Mark Hawthorne

Brilliant, easy to read, full of real-life experiences and practical examples. If you want to make your life count, influence others and save

a few thousand lives, this book is your roadmap. Give it to everyone you know! **Ingrid Newkirk,** president of People for the Ethical Treatment of Animals

9781846940910 304pp **£9.99 $19.95**

Reiki Meditations for Beginners
with free CD
Lawrence Ellyard

One of the few Reiki books which really covers something new and valuable. Reiki and Meditation is a core topic for everyone who likes to use Usui-Reiki as a spiritual path. This is why Mikao Usui emphasized so much to meditate every morning and every evening. A must read for every serious Reiki-Practitioner! **Walter Lübeck,** co-author of *The Spirit of Reiki*

9781846940989 176pp **£12.99 $24.95**

The Celtic Wheel of the Year
Celtic and Christian Seasonal Prayers
Tess Ward

This book is highly recommended. It will make a perfect gift at any time of the year. There is no better way to conclude than by quoting the cover endorsement by Diarmuid O'Murchu MSC, "Tess Ward writes like a mystic. A gem for all seasons!" It is a gem indeed.
Revd. John Churcher, Progressive Christian Network

1905047959 304pp **£11.99 $21.95**

A Global Guide to Interfaith
Reflections From Around the World
Sandy Bharat

This amazing book gives a wonderful picture of the variety and excitement of this journey of discovery.
Rev Dr. Marcus Braybrooke, President of the World Congress of Faiths

1905047975 336pp **£19.99 $34.95**

God in the Bath
Relaxing in the Everywhere Presence of God
Stephen Mitchell

This little book is destined to become a spiritual classic...A wonderfully refreshing and invigorating reading of Christianity.
Nigel Leaves, author of *Odyssey*

1905047657 112pp **£9.99 $19.95**

God Without God
Western Spirituality Without the Wrathful King
Michael Hampson

Writing with an admirable lucidity and following a tight line of argument, Michael Hampson outlines a credible Christian theology for the twenty-first century. Critical at times of both evangelical and catholic traditions, of both liberal and conservative thinking, he seeks to make faith accessible to those for whom established forms of belief have become inappropriate in the present-day context.
Canon David Peacock, former Pro-Rector, University of Surrey

9781846941023 256pp **£9.99 $19.95**